W9-BOM-421

VOTES FOR WOMEN!
The Story of
Carrie Chapman Catt

VOTES FOR WOMEN!
The Story of
Carrie Chapman Catt

Barbara A. Somervill

MORGAN
REYNOLDS
Publishing, Inc.

620 South Elm Street, Suite 223
Greensboro, North Carolina   27406
http://www.morganreynolds.com

036 86547

VOTES FOR WOMEN! THE STORY OF CARRIE CHAPMAN CATT

Library of Congress Cataloging-in-Publication Data

Somervill, Barbara, 1948-
  Votes for women! : the story of Carrie Chapman Catt / Barbara
Somervill.
    p. cm.
Summary: Profiles Carrie Chapman Catt, an educator, prohibitionist, and
women's rights advocate who was instrumental in the passage of the
nineteenth amendment which gave women the right to vote.
Includes bibliographical references and index.
  ISBN 1-883846-96-X
  1. Catt, Carrie Chapman, 1859-1947. 2. Suffragists--United
States--Biography--Juvenile literature. 3. Women in politics--United
States--Biography--Juvenile literature. [1. Catt, Carrie Chapman,
1859-1947. 2. Suffragists. 3. Women--Biography.] I. Title.
  JK1899.C3 S66 2003
  324.6'23'092--dc21

                           2002010358

Printed in the United States of America
First Edition

Feminist Voices

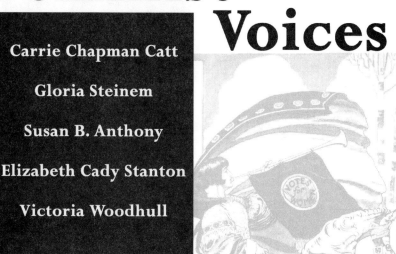

Carrie Chapman Catt

Gloria Steinem

Susan B. Anthony

Elizabeth Cady Stanton

Victoria Woodhull

For MBJ, JAC, and KKM—
three independent-minded women

Contents

Carrie Chapman Catt, 1914
(Courtesy of the Library of Congress.)

Chapter One

Rural Beginnings

When Carrie Lane was only thirteen, she watched as her father prepared to go into town to vote in the presidential election of 1872. At the time, Republican Ulysses S. Grant had decided to run for a second term as president. Grant's success as president was questionable, and many citizens believed the federal government wallowed in corruption. Liberal Republicans and members of the Democratic Party had asked Horace Greeley to oppose Grant in the election. Greeley, best known for his advice "Go West, young man," was a well-known social reformer, newspaper editor, and politician.

Carrie Lane knew all about Horace Greeley. Her parents had actively campaigned for him, and on election day, Carrie's father, Lucius, and the Lane's hired helper went off to vote in the nearby town of Charles City, Iowa.

Carrie asked her mother, Maria, why she, too, did not go to vote. The family laughed at her. Astounded, Carrie learned that women were not allowed to vote. This was the first time that Carrie realized women were legally inferior to men. She had grown up on a farm, where men and women worked equally hard. The thought that her sex made her a "lesser" citizen angered Carrie. This was Carrie Lane's first taste of politics. Although she did not know it at the time, it was an event that would spark a lifelong endeavor for young Carrie.

From her early childhood, Carrie had a strong stubborn streak. If she thought an event was unfair, she fought against it. The struggle for women's voting rights became Carrie's crusade. Those who knew her well were not surprised by the grit and determination she showed in fighting for the right to vote.

Carrie Clinton Lane was born on January 9, 1859, in Ripon, Wisconsin, a little more than two years before the Civil War began. She had an older brother named Charles and a younger brother, Will. As was typical of most families of the time, Lucius worked the farm and provided the family income while Maria kept the home running smoothly. With few modern conveniences in an 1850s farmhouse, Maria's chores were as demanding as plowing and seeding.

During the first six years of Carrie's life, the United States changed dramatically. In late 1860, South Carolina became the first of eleven states to secede from the United States and form the Confederate States of America. In April 1861, Confederate forces fired on Fort Sumter in the harbor outside Charleston, South Carolina. The Civil War had begun.

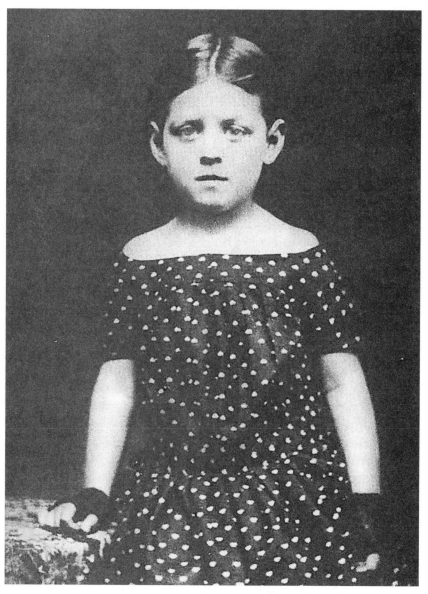

Carrie Lane, age six.
(Courtesy of the Library of Congress.)

Although the Lanes lived far from the fighting, the effects of the Civil War struck every family in Wisconsin. Friends and neighbors left to fight on the Union side. Farms and industries struggled to keep going with reduced labor forces. Fathers fought sons, and brothers fought brothers. The war effected everyone in the United States in some way.

During the war, Congress passed the Homestead Act of 1862, promising free land for those willing to build a home and farm in the West. After the Civil War, the Lanes joined those moving westward and headed for Iowa.

Railroad service stretched as far west as Charles City, Iowa, where the Lanes planned to settle. In 1866, Carrie and her mother arrived by train and set up in temporary lodgings in town. Meanwhile, Lucius and his ten-year-old son, Charles, drove a wagon filled with supplies to the land on which the Lanes would build their farm.

Iowa was much different from heavily wooded Wisconsin. Thick, tall grass filled the flat, open prairie. To protect themselves from the extremes of prairie weather, the Lanes built a large brick home surrounded by a windbreak of fast-growing maple trees. The Lanes brought the trees with them from the East. A stand of trees shaded the house in summer and kept frigid winter winds at bay.

Life on the farm demanded work from every family member. Even at six, Carrie had chores. Spring meant tilling and planting the family's kitchen garden, which

Carrie's mother, Maria Clinton Lane.
(Courtesy of the Library of Congress.)

supplied fresh vegetables in the summer. Fall meant hours of canning—preserving vegetables in jars for the long winter ahead. Cleaning, cooking, feeding live-stock, milking cows, plowing, planting, harvesting, washing clothes, sewing, mending—the list of chores to keep a farm running smoothly seemed endless. Full of energy, Carrie had no problem fitting in schoolwork among her many farm duties. She was greatly skilled at reorganizing a heavy workload into manageable chores. Her time spent doing chores was never wasted. As she milked cows or weeded the vegetable garden, Carrie recited poetry or reviewed her latest history lesson.

Carrie attended school in a one-room schoolhouse near the Lane's farm. Elementary schools in the late 1800s taught basic courses such as reading, writing, and arithmetic. Geography, grammar, and spelling eventually became part of the curriculum. Education in rural districts came a distant second to farming. During plowing, seeding, and harvesting times, children worked on the farm instead of in the schoolhouse. Severe winter weather also kept students from the classroom. The schoolteacher, usually an unmarried woman in her late teens, often had little more education than her students.

Carrie had no problems voicing her opinion or standing up to the boys at school. She developed her own way of coping with bullies. Once, when her brother Charles scared her with a garter snake, she caught her own snake and threw it back at him. Another time, Carrie stood in line with her classmates listening to their teacher. One girl's hoopskirt slipped to the floor, causing the girl bitter embarrassment. The boys decided to tease the unfortunate girl during recess. Carrie walked up to the worst bully of the group and slapped his face—teaching him not to take girls lightly. Early in her teens, Carrie decided she wanted to become a doctor, although few women practiced medicine at the time. Carrie's interest in medicine sprang from two main sources: the abundance of animal specimens available on the Lane farm and a relatively new book, Charles Darwin's *Origin of Species*. Carrie often brought small reptiles and insects into the Lane home and preserved dead animals in her mother's pickling jars. Her father put up with the rodents until Carrie brought home a handful of rattlesnake eggs that began to hatch behind the kitchen stove. This marked the end of her collection. Nevertheless, Carrie found other outlets to appease her inquisitive mind, such as Darwin's books on evolution. Darwin's theory of evolution presented radical ideas distinctly different from the creation story of the Bible. Carrie's mind filled with questions for which she could find few answers.

For Carrie Lane, going to high school required riding five miles on horseback during good weather and boarding with friends during the long, bitter winter months. Although she missed her family, the time she spent in Charles City passed quickly. Tall, blue-eyed Carrie enjoyed a quick wit. Her town friends spoke of her as being mischievous, but she also had a serious side. An avid reader, Carrie memorized long poems that she recited as she did her chores. The longer the task, the longer the poem she chose to keep her mind occupied.

After finishing high school, Carrie hoped that college would fill the blank spaces in her education. Her father, however, had different ideas. He could not understand why Carrie thought she needed a college education. In his mind, a young girl should marry, raise children, and do housework. Carrie was not interested in that kind of life. Determined to go to college, she planned to find a way to pay for her own education.

One opportunity open to young women with a high school education was teaching. Carrie decided she could earn enough money to put herself through college by combining teaching jobs during vacation times with paid housework the rest of the year. She knew teachers were in demand. Young women often taught for a couple of years, but once married, they lost their jobs. Married women were not considered acceptable teachers. Carrie obtained a teaching certificate and worked during the summers.

In 1869, Iowa State Agricultural College opened in Ames, Iowa. Government land grants supported state schools, such as Iowa State, that taught mechanical arts and agriculture. The college proved to be quite a bargain. There was no charge for tuition. Housing cost from one dollar to three dollars and fifty cents per term, and food cost two dollars and fifty cents per week. A no-frills education cost Carrie Lane about $150 per year, which she paid for by teaching, washing dishes for nine cents per hour, and working in the library for ten cents per hour. Finally understanding Carrie's de-

Lucius Lane could not understand why his daughter wanted to attend college.
(Courtesy of the Library of Congress.)

termination to further her education, her father offered to pay twenty-five dollars per year toward her expenses. Two required courses Carrie studied at Ames were domestic economy and domestic chemistry. The first seemed almost laughable to Carrie because most married women could not legally own anything. Their money, land, household goods, and even wages belonged to their husbands. In other words, domestic economy taught women how to carefully handle money even though they had none. Domestic chemistry, on the other hand, explained how to make soap, candles, detergents, and furniture polish to use for household chores such as cleaning and doing laundry. Neither of those subjects appealed to Carrie.

Carrie became a leading force in changing attitudes toward female students at her school. She initiated two major changes at Iowa State. First, she started a women's military training program similar to the already existing drill for the men. A course in military training was offered for all men at land grant colleges. Drill provided healthy exercise and discipline, according to General Geddes, who ran the program. Carrie proposed that Geddes offer the same healthy program for women. Although he initially laughed at the idea, Geddes saw that Carrie had a valid point, and Company G (for girls) was formed. A regular drill program for Company G continued through World War I.

Carrie's second accomplishment involved the university literary society. She challenged the society to allow female students to become more active. The literary society encouraged students to read various works by authors and poets and then discuss those works in a group. The rules of the society allowed men to give speeches, but women could only write their ideas in essay form. This was not enough for Carrie, who insisted on giving speeches herself. A discussion on women's voting rights caused Carrie to break her silence. From this point on, women could speak at the literary society meetings.

Carrie's speaking skills blossomed. In her first year at Ames, she spoke at a teacher's school about the importance of providing women with a solid education. She believed that educated women were better prepared to raise children, and she related this idea to women's voting. Many men felt women simply lacked the brainpower to vote. Carrie asked, "How is it possible that a woman who is unfit to vote, should be the mother of, and bring up, a man who is?"

At the Iowa State commencement ceremony in 1880, Carrie graduated with a degree in General Science for Women, similar to a degree in home economics with added general science. Bright and ambitious, she was the only female graduate in her class.

Carrie hoped to become a lawyer after college, a new profession for women at that time. She worked briefly in a law office until she was offered a teaching job in Mason City, Iowa. In March 1883, Carrie seized an opportunity to advance her career. The man who served as both principal of Carrie's school and superintendent of schools in Mason City gave up his job. Students unanimously petitioned for Carrie to fill the position, and despite mild skepticism that a woman could serve as superintendent, she was offered the job.

Some critics doubted that twenty-four-year-old Carrie could succeed as superintendent. She quickly proved them wrong. On her first day in the job, she addressed a serious problem in the Mason City schools: truancy, or skipping school. She went from school to school, pulling the worst truancy offenders from class and slapping a heavy leather strap across their backs. By the end of the day, every student knew better than to cut school. One student said, "We were . . . twice as big as Carrie Lane, but we never questioned her authority."

As superintendent, Carrie encouraged students studying English to write school news articles for local newspapers. She first approached the *Mason City Republican*, edited by Leo Chapman. Carrie's appeal to Chapman to print school news in his paper succeeded beyond her wildest dreams.

Chapman, an avid supporter of the temperance movement and woman suffrage, was impressed by Carrie's education and manner. Chapman pursued Carrie socially. The two were soon engaged to be married, despite Carrie's negative view of marriage. However, Leo did not expect her to give up her job to wash, clean, and raise children.

On February 12, 1885, Carrie Lane and Leo Chapman married at the Lane farm. The *Floyd County Advocate* printed details of the ceremony, including this prediction of the couple's future:

Carrie (center), pictured here with her teaching colleagues, applied for the position of superintendent of Mason City schools. *(Courtesy of the Library of Congess.)*

Few young people start out in life with better capabilities and larger promise of success than do Mr. and Mrs. Chapman, and a wide circle of friends are earnest in their wishes that their brightest dreams may be realized. It is understood that the bride will assist her husband in the literary work on his paper, in which the *Republican* will be far better equipped for ability than most county papers.

Chapter Two

Lighting a Fire

In the autumn after her marriage, Carrie Lane Chapman spent three days on assignment in Des Moines, Iowa. She was there to cover a three-day meeting of the American Association of Women. The meeting's speakers included female lawyers, college professors, doctors, and journalists. Topics ranged from woman suffrage to temperance to legal rights of women—of which there were few in 1885. Carrie was in awe. She listened to women's rights activists speak, including nationally famous suffragist Lucy Stone.

Inspired by these women, Carrie Chapman entered the political arena for the first time that fall. She ran for county superintendent of schools in the primary elections. Her main opponent, Henry Shepard, had a long political history, having served for a number of years as county auditor. When Shepard became the Republican candidate for superintendent, Leo Chapman wrote an editorial accusing Shepard of using county money in a scam.

Shepard won the election, and then he sued Chapman for libel. The judge hearing the case was a close friend of Shepard's, and the libel suit went against Leo Chapman. The loss forced the Chapmans to sell their newspaper.

Leo headed to San Francisco in search of work while Carrie stayed with her parents. Three months after he left, Carrie received a telegram informing her that Leo had contracted typhoid fever. She left by train to join him, but by the time she reached San Francisco, her husband of little more than a year had already died.

Life for the widowed Mrs. Chapman grew increasingly difficult. She had no money to fall back on, no job, no home, and she thought, no future. Luckily, Carrie had an aunt in San Francisco who offered her a place to live.

Throughout the next year, Carrie worked as the first female journalist for a San Francisco paper. This was not a full-time job, but one that paid only for articles the paper printed. The articles paid very little money, and she barely scraped by.

Women who worked outside the home in the late 1880s struggled against major obstacles. They received low pay for long hours, along with the threat of losing their jobs if they complained. Working women found few higher paying jobs available to them. They often experienced sexual harassment by employers.

Carrie experienced all the worst of a working woman's life. She sold ads for the newspaper, wrote articles, and worked endlessly. She earned money only

Leo Chapman died shortly after he and Carrie were married.
(Courtesy of the Library of Congress.)

when she sold ads or articles, which meant that her income varied from week to week. Carrie's editor saw her as easy prey. One evening, he grabbed her in his office, kissing her and fondling her body. She fought him off but was left sickened and humiliated. Realizing the pain that many women dealt with, she resolved to improve the fortunes of working women.

Carrie believed that the first step in achieving equality was suffrage, or gaining women the right to vote. Without the vote, women could not influence lawmakers or force social change. Reform movements played an active political role throughout the 1800s, but change came slowly and only with great effort.

Long before Carrie was born, three major social movements became the focal points of women's reform efforts: abolition, temperance, and suffrage. Abolitionists hoped to bring an end to slavery. The temperance movement sought to end the manufacture and sale of alcoholic drinks, and suffrage would give women the right to vote. Each of these three movements concerned the rights of women, although in very different ways.

The antislavery, or abolition, movement began as early as 1775 with the founding of the first antislavery society in Philadelphia. The goals of abolitionists varied. Some wanted to end slavery completely. Others only hoped to stop the spread of slavery to new territories in the United States. Still others saw abolition and women's rights as closely allied causes, because slaves and women lacked similar freedoms under the white male-oriented laws of the 1800s. Just as a master owned a slave, a husband possessed his wife and all her belongings. Powerful people rose up in support of abolition. Among them were William Lloyd Garrison, Frederick Douglass, Harriet Beecher Stowe, Lucretia Mott, and Elizabeth Cady Stanton. Garrison edited *The Liberator,* a small, influential journal that promoted his antislavery sentiments. Frederick Douglass, an African American who had escaped from slavery, spoke avidly about the plight of slaves. Both men also favored women's rights, although they focused on abolition. Women participated in the antislavery efforts, but they were sometimes dismissed because of their sex. At the World's Anti-slavery Convention, held in London, England, in 1840, Mott and Stanton were barred from the meeting because they were female.

The temperance movement was a nationwide effort to stop the manufacture and sale of alcoholic drinks. Many men drank their wages away while their families starved. Women suffered from violence at the hands of drunken husbands and relatives. Temperance activists believed these problems would be solved if the supply of alcoholic beverages dried up.

At the center of the temperance movement stood the Women's Christian Temperance Union (WCTU), founded in 1874 in Cleveland, Ohio. Annie Wittenmyer, Frances Willard, and Anna Howard Shaw led the group, which promoted temperance through education. The WCTU also supported prison reform and woman suffrage. Dr. Shaw, a minister, would later become a major player in the suffrage movement. The first Women's Rights Convention in the United States met in Seneca Falls, New York, in July 1848. At this meeting, activists set the primary goals for women. For the next dozen years, women's rights activists met yearly to discuss progress and make plans. These women believed that voting equaled political power. The only way they could change laws that deprived women of equal rights was through voting for sympathetic lawmakers and against those who opposed women's rights.

The suffrage effort suffered a serious setback when the Civil War began. Interest in women's rights fell as both the North and South concentrated on the war effort. At the end of the war, Elizabeth Cady Stanton and Susan B. Anthony formed the American Equal Rights Association, a group promoting the vote for white women and all adult African Americans.

In 1868, the Fourteenth Amendment to the Constitution was ratified, striking a damaging blow to the woman suffrage movement. This amendment protected all citizens against unfair state laws, then went on to define both "citizens" and "voters" as male. Women's rights activists were furious.

Within the women's rights movement, two separate factions arose over whether or not to support suffrage for African Americans. In 1869, Lucy Stone founded the American Woman Suffrage Association (AWSA), to help get African Americans the vote. Woman suffrage could come after African-American suffrage, they proposed. Stone's followers included a number of famous

Susan B. Anthony led the fight for women's rights, along with Elizabeth Cady Stanton, Lucy Stone, Lucretia Mott, and others. *(Courtesy of the Library of Congress.)*

abolitionists, including William Lloyd Garrison and Henry Blackwell. When Stone and Blackwell married, Stone decided not to take her husband's last name as her own. Throughout her life she was known as Lucy Stone, an avid abolitionist and women's rights activist. Overall, Stone's AWSA believed that woman suffrage held only a small place in the greater scheme of social reform. AWSA supporters favored a slow, gradual increase of women's rights, including voting, property ownership, and personal freedoms.

That same year, Elizabeth Cady Stanton and Susan B. Anthony started the National Woman Suffrage Association (NWSA) dedicated solely to winning the vote for women. The NWSA took a more radical approach to women's rights, even showing compassion for divorced women—a shocking viewpoint at that time. Anthony proposed an aggressive strategy for winning the vote. Her view was to force the issue, thrusting woman suffrage in the collective faces of the U.S. Congress as often as possible.

By 1886, Carrie Chapman was drawn again to social reform. Her husband's death and her experience as a working woman drove her to action. Her own situation demanded that she do something to improve her status and that of other working women. The abolition question had been answered, but the issues of temperance, women's rights, and suffrage stood out in the minds of progressive thinkers. In San Francisco, Carrie struggled to earn enough money to survive. She quickly realized that she would have to take action in order to support herself.

Around that time, a man named George Catt came into Carrie's life. Catt remembered Carrie as a fellow student at Iowa State. He was surprised to see Carrie walking down the street one day in San Francisco. Catt worked there as an engineer. The two became friends, with Catt pursuing Carrie in hopes of eventually marrying her.

After spending time with Catt, Carrie realized that she could have greater financial success on a speaking tour than she had selling ads for a newspaper. Carrie liked the idea of speaking. She quickly came up with three lectures, hired an agent, and set off to make her name as a public speaker.

Carrie knew that she would have better luck working from Charles City, Iowa, where her family was known, than from San Francisco. After practicing her speeches on the West Coast a few times, she moved back to Iowa.

Carrie's lecture topics covered typical interests of the time. The first was "Zenobia," an historic narrative about the queen of Palmyra and her fate before the Roman emperor. The second lecture, titled "A True Story," described a young girl's tragic situation as a Chinese child sold into prostitution and shipped to San Francisco, and the lack of legal help available to her. The last lecture, "America for Americans," had a distinctively anti-immigrant flavor.

The lecture circuit paid well, but Carrie often found herself staying in uncomfortable lodgings, missing meals, and traveling long hours on trains. Speakers' fees ranged from ten dollars to twenty-five dollars per speech. In her first four months as a speaker, Carrie earned just over one hundred dollars. From this money, she paid ten dollars monthly for her house in Charles City, along with paying for food, coal for heating, and household goods. Food was cheap—steak at ten cents per pound, butter for twenty cents per pound. Carrie's earnings did not go far enough to provide any luxuries, but life had improved dramatically from her hit-or-miss earnings in San Francisco.

In 1887, the U.S. Senate voted on woman suffrage. The proposed amendment lost: thirty-four votes against to sixteen votes in favor. Two dozen senators considered the issue either too politically explosive or too uninspiring to even bother voting. The suffrage movement suffered a setback but rallied with new strategies. Suffragists planned to develop strong, active local groups that could promote the women's vote on a state-by-state basis.

Carrie Chapman's speaking talent brought her to the attention of the Iowa Woman Suffrage Association. In 1889, the group's leader, Margaret Campbell, asked Chapman to become the state organizer and recording secretary. She would receive a small salary. As such, Carrie would travel from town to town to organize support for woman suffrage. Organization was a road to leadership for Carrie, and she therefore agreed, even though money would be tight. This would give Carrie more chances to deliver her lectures and also to fight for woman suffrage. The more Carrie worked with the association, the greater recognition they returned to her as a fellow woman suffragist. This rapport sparked energy in Carrie to take on a stronger role in the suffrage crusade.

As part of her job, she set up a system for collecting money to support the association's needs. She immediately formed the first chapter of the Political Equality Club in Sioux City, Iowa. Within a year, Chapman developed ten such clubs. During this time, Carrie gained the valuable organizational skills and speaking experience she needed to step into the national suffrage arena.

Chapter Three

A Time of Change

The year 1890 brought great changes for both the woman suffrage movement and Carrie Chapman. In February 1890, the AWSA and the NWSA put aside their differences and joined together to form the National American Woman Suffrage Association (NAWSA). Chapman, on a lecture tour of the East Coast, found herself near enough to Washington, D.C., to attend the conference.

By 1890, the founders of the women's movement were aging and exhausted from years of fighting for women's rights. The mother of suffrage, Susan B. Anthony, turned seventy that year. Lucy Stone had reached seventy-two. The eldest of the great activists, Elizabeth Cady Stanton, was then seventy-four. Carrie respected the work done by these three women, although she knew them more by reputation than through personal contact. Carrie saw that it was time for new people, new ideas, and new strategies to take their places in the suffrage movement.

At the conference in Washington, D.C., Carrie Chapman spoke before the association for the first time. Her speech was entitled "The Symbol of Liberty." Although Chapman offered no startling ideas in her speech, it was her delivery that moved the crowd. Her bold charisma as a speaker, her command of the audience, and her ability to clearly explain a concept immediately boosted her popularity. Carrie Chapman had suddenly stepped into national fame.

Shortly after the national conference, Carrie headed to Seattle for her second wedding. She married George Catt in a small, private ceremony in their home. Unaware that Carrie had planned to marry, Iowa suffrage leaders and friends assumed that marriage meant the end of Carrie's work. They could not have been more wrong. They had no idea that George Catt not only agreed with Carrie's work, but he also intended to support her efforts. Rumors circulated that Carrie and George created a contract that allowed Carrie to work for woman suffrage four months out of each year.

Carrie Chapman Catt described her marriage in this way: "We made a team to work for the cause. My husband used to say that he was as much a reformer as I, but that he couldn't work at reforming and earn a living at the same time; but what he could do was earn a living enough for two and free me from all economic burden, and thus I could reform for two. That was our bargain and we happily understood each other."

Within a few months of her marriage, Carrie Chapman Catt headed to South Dakota for her first major suffrage campaign. The state suffrage association hoped to add an amendment to the South Dakota state constitution that would allow women to vote in state elections.

The hardships of Carrie's earlier speaking tours barely compared with her adventures in South Dakota. She was devastated to learn of the desolate conditions in South Dakota from years of drought. Her first speaking engagement took place in a granary, a silo for storing grain. There was no "town" to speak of, just the granary, a railroad platform, and a tiny post office. Carrie spent the night in the postmaster's home, sharing a bed with his daughter. The only available restroom was an outhouse.

Carrie found that this stop provided luxuries greater than many others during her tour of South Dakota. At one train stop, she saw nothing other than the train platform and a silo—not a house, tree, bush, or person for miles. Carrie waited for several hours until a farmer arrived to take her to her speaking engagement. Again, she stayed overnight in a farmhouse. The attic served as the family bedroom with five large double beds. Carrie shared a bed with the local schoolteacher.

Times were hard on South Dakota farm families, and Carrie experienced some of those difficulties. "At one place where I took three meals, I had bread and watermelon and tea for each meal and the people themselves had not had anything else for a long time."

The suffrage meetings were well attended, but Carrie took a realistic view of the potential for victory. She

Carrie and George Catt agreed to pursue the fight for woman suffrage together.
(Courtesy of the Library of Congress.)

anticipated winning only twenty thousand votes in favor of woman suffrage, a number too low to ensure victory. On election day, Carrie's assessment proved accurate. The amendment failed with forty-five thousand votes against and twenty-two thousand votes in favor.

Carrie became frustrated when she saw first-hand the dishonesty of the South Dakota voters. As she watched the polls, she saw a number of young men enter the voting booths with large groups of non-English-speaking male voters. Because the voters could not read the ballots, the young men marked the ballots for them, casting their votes in opposition of woman suffrage. As each non-English-speaking man left the polling booth, he received cash from the young men for his vote. Carrie felt great anger knowing that the vote for woman suffrage lost because of improper voting:

> Not one of them could speak English or sign his name in any language. And when they voted . . . the lead . . . would hand over to these men one dollar and sometimes two dollars in plain sight. Through this Russian-German element under the leadership of somebody who had money to pay to defeat woman suffrage, it went down to defeat.

Carrie learned several valuable lessons from the South Dakota defeat. Future campaigns needed support by major citizens' groups and political parties, a reasonable supply of money, and organized, determined campaigners. She made a promise to herself to fight even harder for the next campaign. The South Dakota campaign left Carrie exhausted. She traveled with her husband to San Francisco, where she contracted typhoid fever, the same disease that had killed Leo Chapman less than five years earlier. For two months, Carrie struggled against the illness. Although she was weak and listless, Carrie still managed to travel somewhat and give her speeches. Regaining her full health took months.

George Catt's engineering business grew, and soon the couple moved east to keep up with his work. In 1891, George and Carrie moved to Boston, Massachusetts, settling in a temporary home near the Stone-Blackwell family. The Stone-Blackwell family's place in the suffrage movement attracted Carrie's interest.

Lucy Stone no longer took an active part in the movement. Her age and frailty prevented her from editing *The Woman's Journal,* the magazine she started to support the AWSA. Lucy's daughter Alice had taken over that task and brought new life and a distinct literary flair to the writing. Carrie admired both women. She became a frequent visitor to the Stone-Blackwell home and a close friend to Alice Stone Blackwell.

At the February 1892 NAWSA conference in Washington, D.C., Elizabeth Cady Stanton and Lucy Stone retired as president and vice president of the national organization. Susan B. Anthony became the new president, but at seventy-three years old, Anthony's age limited her. Energetic young activists stepped in to support

Anthony at every level of the suffrage movement.

Anthony realized Carrie's potential to the suffrage organization and asked her to chair a business committee for NAWSA. This allowed Carrie the opportunity to really put her organizational skills to use. Her responsibilities included finding suffragists through other lecturers, hiring speakers, organizing their trips, and raising money.

Shortly after the convention, Carrie and George moved once again, this time to a permanent home in Brooklyn, New York. Although she was now a New Yorker, Carrie maintained close ties to suffragists in Iowa. Together they organized the Mississippi Valley Suffrage Conference in Des Moines, Iowa. Anxious to work with other activists who could not attend the conferences in Washington, Carrie set up the Mississippi Valley conference to give these women a chance to meet and discuss new ideas. Susan B. Anthony was among the national suffragists to attend the meeting.

At the time when Carrie became an officer in NAWSA, only Wyoming allowed women to vote. Then, at the Columbian Exposition in Chicago in 1893, Ellis Meredith, a reporter for the *Rocky Mountain News* in Denver, Colorado, approached Susan B. Anthony about organizing a campaign in Colorado. When Anthony refused, Meredith turned to Carrie. Although hesitant at first because of financial woes, Carrie decided to help Meredith.

Colorado's legislature had passed a law giving women the vote, but that law had to be approved by the voters.

Alice Stone Blackwell edited *The Woman's Journal. (Courtesy of the Library of Congress.)*

A special election, called a referendum, would be held in the fall of 1893. There was no state or federal election in Colorado that year; therefore political parties would not be actively campaigning against the suffrage issue. In addition, a financial depression had Colorado voters looking for political change, which came via the Populist Party. The Populists were a loose political alliance that focused on agricultural issues, such as economic aid to farmers. The Populists supported woman suffrage.

This was a chance for Carrie Chapman Catt to put

her great organizational skills to work. She immediately promised her support and planned the campaign's strategies. As part of Carrie's plan, the suffragists kept their campaign as quiet as possible. The more publicity they received, the more likely the opposition would rise against them. Instead, maintaining a low profile would prevent the movement's greatest enemies from organizing a counter-campaign.

Carrie quickly developed several layers of support, including speakers, meeting organizers, fund-raisers, and door-to-door campaigners. She herself spoke at every occasion, from a watermelon festival to a miners' meeting.

On one occasion, Carrie found herself stuck in Silverton, Colorado, needing to get to a meeting in another town. She planned to travel by train, only to discover that an accident on the tracks had stopped all travel down the mountain. The only alternative was to ride a handcar on the train tracks.

A one-armed man agreed to operate the handcar, bringing the car's "brakes"—a wooden board—with him. Carrie sat on the car's platform, her feet supported by a loop of rope, and a package of sandwiches in her lap. With a quick push from the ticket agent, the cart headed downhill. As their speed increased, Carrie held on for dear life. The sandwiches flew off her lap, and she clutched her hat to her chest. Approaching the wreck, the one-armed operator shoved the board against the rails. Amid a dreadful squeal and the smell of burning wood, the cart finally stopped.

Several hours later, Carrie arrived at her destination. Intent upon hearing their gracious speaker, the audience had waited for Carrie. The harrowing experience of the flight on the pushcart behind her, she stood before the crowd and boasted of the importance of woman suffrage. With Carrie's enthusiasm and sharp skills, the Colorado campaign turned out to be a great success. The financial costs were low—a mere nineteen hundred dollars—and woman suffrage passed by more than six thousand votes. Only three out of the twenty-nine counties that Carrie had visited voted in opposition to woman suffrage. NAWSA added a second victory to their battle, with Carrie Chapman Catt as the leader of the victory campaign. Carrie described the event in glowing terms:

> Startled by their own victory, the women wanted to do something in celebration which would remain forever after in their memories. A crowd gathered in the suffrage headquarters and they talked it over, but being unable to devise any unique plan, some one started 'Praise God from whom all blessings flow,' and people passing by outside heard a great chorus of song. After which the tired workers went home quietly with praise God singing in their hearts.

Chapter Four

Learning to Lead

Spurred on by the thrill of Carrie's victory in Colorado, NAWSA planned campaigns in New York and Kansas. Once again, opposition rose up against the suffragists.

In New York, the legislature was creating a new state constitution in 1894. Suffragists demanded that it include woman suffrage. Carrie traveled throughout New York to deliver speeches encouraging others to advocate for women's voting rights. Farmers and labor unions comprised the largest group of supporters.

Opposition to the amendment came from several sources, including both men and women. Those opposed argued that the right to vote carried with it the obligation to bear arms, which women could not do. Others reasoned that women held an inferior position in the world, based on the Bible. Still others argued that women did not really want to vote. Due to the small number of suffragists in the state, Carrie herself was especially weary. One of the most insulting viewpoints held that women were born weaker than men and lacked the ability to make strong, rational decisions. Carrie considered these arguments absurd. They only drove her to fight harder. The *New York Times* quoted Carrie as saying, "The ballot is the weapon women need for protection and advancement, whether they use it or not."

The New York suffrage campaign stalled before it ever got moving. On the suffrage side, committees collected six hundred thousand signatures on a petition to add a suffrage amendment to the state constitution. A petition with fifteen thousand signatures opposed the addition. The politicians on the convention's suffrage committee agreed with the viewpoint supported by the shorter petition. They simply ignored the petition with six hundred thousand signatures and dropped the amendment.

Suffragists thought that Kansas, a rural state with a strong Populist following, would offer a good opportunity because of the powerful suffrage movement there. Women could already vote in municipal and school elections. That same year, Carrie Chapman Catt, Susan B. Anthony, and Anna Howard Shaw arrived in Kansas early in the campaign to lend their support. They organized a comprehensive campaign that reached as many people as possible in the state.

The political situation in Kansas caused the campaign's undoing. At the time, Populists, Republicans, and Democrats all fought to gain power in the largely agricultural state. In other states, Populists openly supported woman suffrage. Republicans did not want to take on any controversial issues at the risk of losing voters, while Democrats wanted to become more powerful and therefore took no stance at all on the issue. In Kansas, politicians worried about every issue that might lose their parties even a single vote. No Kansas political party would take a chance on losing voters by supporting woman suffrage.

The political upheaval in Kansas soon fell apart. Farm income fell as a financial depression swept through the state. When the Populists met to develop their platform for the fall elections, many party members refused to discuss woman suffrage. Only after heavy lobbying forced the issue would the Populists grudgingly support suffrage. Unfortunately, they did so with a postscript saying that the party did not expect its members to uphold the idea.

The political atmosphere grew heated. As Carrie quickly moved from town to town, she found herself always at odds with one group or another. If she spoke to Populists, no Republicans or Democrats attended the meeting. Likewise, when she spoke to Republicans, Carrie saw no Populists or Democrats. Nevertheless, her speaking skills and vivacious attitude captured audiences in a way that few suffrage speakers could.

The Woman's Journal, Alice Stone Blackwell's suffrage magazine, reported Carrie's success with the campaign:

The largest auditorium in the city was packed both nights, many men stood for three hours and many others failed to get in. Carrie was new to Topeka and spoke at a late hour, but she captured her hearers as she always does everywhere . . . It is suggested . . . for her to address voters only, as they are being crowded out by the many women who attend these meetings.

Carrie spoke in 103 of the total 105 Kansas counties. Her stamina and endurance were often tested, particularly in traveling through the state. Once, in the sparsely populated western part of Kansas, Carrie had no way to reach her destination for a speaking engagement. No trains traveled to the town, and no stagecoach was scheduled to make the trip. Carrie found herself in a situation similar to the one she had been in during her Colorado campaign. Unwilling to give up, Carrie rented a wagon and team of horses, asked for directions, and finally set off on her own. She had often had to fend for herself, and this was no exception. The trip involved many turns, and the flat, bleak Kansas landscape provided no landmarks to guide her. Four hours later, Carrie arrived in the town, to the surprise of herself and her hostesses.

This incident showed a great deal about Carrie's character. When she committed herself to a cause, she gave it her full effort. Broken trains, limited transportation, and lack of money soon became tedious challenges that Carrie overcame as part of her daily work. With hardships such as these, many women gave up the suffrage cause, but Carrie firmly marched on with an open and hopeful mind.

The Kansas campaign illustrated the problem of suffragists' winning the battle but losing the war. The suffrage amendment failed by thirty-five thousand votes. Carrie, who had worked tirelessly traveling to promote the amendment, considered it, "the most heart-breaking defeat of the suffrage struggle." Most Kansas voters actually favored woman suffrage, yet they cast their votes to sway political power to a friend or against another party. Months of effort and thousands of dollars fell to another painful defeat for the suffrage movement.

Rigorous campaigning took its toll on Carrie's health. Exhausted and weary, she returned home to rest and recuperate after months on the road. Just as she had recited poetry through her many chores as a child, she turned her mind to planning future campaigns as she worked around the house.

Recalling her early years on the family farm made Carrie happy. At home, she loved working in the kitchen. She spent hours cooking, canning, and planning dinners for her husband and their friends. Carrie welcomed with open arms anyone willing to work for woman suffrage. The Catt home became a "headquarters" for suffrage activists in the New York City area. She, George, and their friends spent many evenings in lively conversation over dinner where they planned campaigns, rehashed failures, and analyzed successes. However, Carrie's time spent at home was all too short. Suffrage work took her away again as soon as she had rested from the Kansas defeat.

In 1895, the annual NAWSA convention was slated for Atlanta. The South, a traditionally male-dominated region, had not been tackled before, and Susan B. Anthony planned to sweep through that region.

Carrie traveled with seventy-five-year-old Anthony throughout Kentucky, Tennessee, Louisiana, and Alabama. The two women had very different ideas about Carrie's duties during the campaign. Anthony considered Carrie to be her companion and organizer, while Carrie thought her own job was to finish Anthony's speeches. Anthony's age limited her ability to carry out such a heavy schedule, and she often tired a third of the way into her after-dinner speeches. She would take her seat, and Carrie continued where Anthony left off. Anthony often spent much of her speech scolding the males in the audience, but when Carrie had her turn to speak, she took a more diplomatic approach.

Although they worked well as team, Anthony and Carrie held opposing views about men in the suffrage movement. Anthony, after years of campaigning and fighting for fair treatment, grew angry with the men attending her meetings. Although many men supported woman suffrage, Anthony often scolded all men for their failure to aid the suffrage cause. Carrie thought that a cynical, angry approach was counterproductive. Instead, she complimented the male members of the audience, assuming that they favored woman suffrage. This often won her a better rapport with the audience.

Throughout their tour, Carrie and Anthony were often welcomed at African-American churches and meetings. Their acceptance by the African-American community hurt their image among the white population. Although the Civil War had ended thirty years earlier, segregation laws, known as Jim Crow laws, had been passed throughout the South. The laws mandated separate schools, restaurants, rest rooms, and seating on trains for African Americans. Carrie and Anthony approached everyone as equals, but many Southerners did not accept this viewpoint.

Carrie and Anthony ended their southern tour with the 1894 NAWSA convention in Atlanta, the first convention held outside Washington, D.C. The main meeting took place in Atlanta's Opera House, with Anthony introducing women to one another and making witty jokes. Carrie was nervous about the suffrage movement depending on the social skills of one elderly woman. "Suffrage is today the strongest reform there is in this country, but it is represented by the weakest organization," Carrie said at the convention. Eager to make bigger and better accomplishments in the suffrage movement, Carrie proposed a number of changes in NAWSA's structure. Because she knew that what the association needed most was organization, she formed the NAWSA Organization Committee.

As the committee was Carrie's idea, the NAWSA board appointed her to lead the group. The committee managed a budget of five thousand dollars a year and would plan and coordinate all suffrage campaigns throughout the country. It eventually became one of the defining groups of the suffrage movement. As head of the organization, Carrie took on more responsibility than she ever had before. Enthusiastic to get started, Carrie came up with dozens of creative ideas. The first was to provide seminars to educate women about politics. She also set up a speaker's bureau, supplying knowledgeable speakers to meetings nationwide.

For lack of money, the committee met in the Catt household. They wrote letters, sent telegrams, and plotted state campaigns. In good weather, the committee held meetings in the backyard. Carrie provided homemade cake and lemonade. The committee seemed casual and comfortable, but with the leadership of Carrie, their accomplishments were many.

Carrie had the idea to prove that women were victims of taxation without representation. To this end, suffrage workers pored over the tax lists of major population centers, compiling an accurate list of the dollar value of taxes paid by women. These women, Carrie advocated, pulled their weight in society, just like men, but they were not accorded the same rights.

One of the main responsibilities of Carrie's Organization Committee was planning suffrage campaigns. They identified key target states and territories, most of which were in the West. Success in Wyoming and Colorado could possibly generate success in other western states. Carrie realized that women and men shared work on western ranches and farms, and therefore their family situations showed women and men on a more equal level than in the East. Carrie also thought that new states just joining the Union might be more accepting of woman suffrage than the conservative states in the East.

Carrie toured the western states in the fall, meeting with local and state suffrage workers to determine the potential for success in each state. The next state to debate woman suffrage was Utah. In 1895, polygamy, or having more than one spouse, still flourished in the mainly Mormon state. Few suffragists, including Carrie, held out much hope for a positive outcome. Acquainted with few people in Utah, Carrie decided not to visit the state. Instead, she left the campaigning up to one individual, Emmeline Wells. Wells, a sharp and dynamic woman from Utah, wrote for and edited a Mormon woman's journal. After going to a national suffrage association meeting in 1879, Wells had become an advocate for the cause.

Emmeline Wells organized the state according to Carrie's general plans. By 1895, sparsely populated Utah claimed more suffragists than highly populated New York. When Utah submitted its state constitution for approval, the document contained woman suffrage. On January 4, 1896, Utah became the forty-fifth state in the Union, and the third state to grant all women the right to vote.

Carrie's hectic schedule allowed little time for family life. A suffrage advocate himself, George Catt often traveled with Carrie, attending a number of conven-

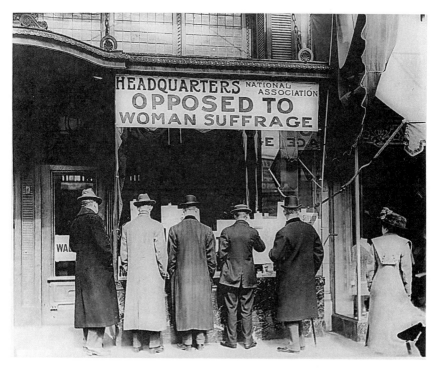

The National Anti-Suffrage Association opposed the work of reformers such as Carrie Chapman Catt. *(Courtesy of the Library of Congress.)*

tions and conferences. His work continued to flourish, and the Catts enjoyed a comfortable lifestyle. Carrie often credited George's generosity for her ability to support the suffrage movement with so much time and energy. His premarital commitment to support them both while Carrie worked for the suffrage movement lasted throughout their lives together.

At one point, the Catts decided to improve suffrage campaigns in the West by offering financial support to suffrage associations. Carrie hoped this would increase the size of the associations. The Catts encouraged other associations to boost their memberships by offering a cash incentive. They paid money to every group that substantially built its membership.

By 1896, Carrie had led the Organization Committee to increase the number of suffrage organizations from seven hundred to eight hundred in just one year. Members wrote letters by the thousand. They printed brochures, visited clubs, and worked with states that needed help in their campaigns.

Money became a major issue. The Organization Committee's initial budget provided only five thousand dollars. Carrie needed more help, more supplies, and obviously, more money. To earn the needed resources, Carrie started a shopping agency, developed a suffrage calendar for the committee to sell, and asked for contributions. By the end of the year, she had raised an additional five thousand dollars.

The committee's efforts had grown to the point that it could no longer work out of the Catt household. The Organization Committee set up offices in the same New York City building in which George Catt's company worked. While NAWSA as a whole continued to seek contributions, the great majority of money brought in to the suffrage movement came to Carrie and the Organization Committee.

Another presidential election would occur in 1896, and the suffrage movement needed to make the most of the political fervor of the moment. The Republicans planned a national convention in St. Louis, while the

Democrats would meet in Chicago. Carrie decided to attend both as part of a suffrage delegation, hoping to sway the parties to include woman suffrage in their election platforms. Republicans were willing to accept female assistance in the election, but they had no intention of supporting female voting rights. The Democratic Party's disinterest in woman suffrage equaled that of the Republicans'.

On a state level, Idaho and California both had suffrage amendment campaigns in action during the year. The greater campaign took place in California, where suffrage leaders remained hopeful up until a few days before the election.

For months, Carrie, Anna Howard Shaw, Susan B. Anthony, and other women's rights leaders traveled through California, speaking to everyone who would sit down long enough to listen. California's size meant that Catt, Shaw, and Anthony spent a great deal of their campaign time traveling. Now in her late seventies, Anthony tired easily. Carrie, who always gave her best effort, exhausted herself. Nevertheless, she kept up a cheerful optimism about the movement's hope for success in California.

They met almost no organized opposition until barely a week before the election. Newspapers in San Francisco, Oakland, and Alameda—all in northern California—printed editorials strongly against the woman suffrage amendment.

On election day, a massive number of Chinese-American voters arrived at the polling places. As Carrie

watched the poll booths, she sadly realized that the
same situation that had happened years before in South
Dakota was now happening again. In response, Carrie
exclaimed:

> Faithful watchers reported that these men were rarely
> informed enough to mark more than one item on the
> ballot, in which case their vote was invariably marked
> against the amendment . . . By a curious cynicism,
> Chinese voters now, with the possible knowledge of
> those who had once protested against them and cer-
> tainly with the aid of their fellow partisans, directed
> their votes to deny self-government to American
> women. It was the hour of the Chinese!

The combined votes of San Francisco, Oakland, and
Alameda defeated the woman suffrage amendment in
California. Idaho, on the other hand, had all four political parties supporting woman suffrage. Although little
time and even less money was spent on the campaign,
the amendment passed by almost six thousand votes.

Despite the loss in California, Carrie continued to
pursue her goals with energy and enthusiasm. Her personal strength did not allow her to cave in under defeat.
She would simply try harder the next time.

During 1897, Carrie's Organization Committee raised
more money than NAWSA as a whole. Extensive campaigns ran in Mississippi, Tennessee, Maryland, Mis-
souri, and West Virginia. In all, more than one thousand
meetings took place to promote suffrage, organize new

suffrage clubs, and lobby politicians. The fight continued, and Carrie Chapman Catt became one of the gener-
als plotting each campaign as though it were a battle
plan.

Chapter Five

Madam President

In 1900, Susan B. Anthony celebrated her eightieth birthday. The respected and honored woman sadly realized it was time to step down as president of NAWSA, but the choice of a replacement concerned her.

Three candidates came to mind among the association's membership. Dr. Anna Howard Shaw, a follower and supporter of Susan B. Anthony, desperately wanted the job. Lillie Devereux Blake, a protégé of Elizabeth Cady Stanton, also ran for the position. Of course, the chairwoman of the Organization Committee, Carrie Chapman Catt, deserved consideration.

Shaw believed herself to be the best candidate, and the one Anthony would certainly select as her successor. Dr. Anna Howard Shaw, however, was unmarried and relied on fees from speaking tours to support herself. The presidency of NAWSA provided no salary—only expenses—and would have been a hardship on Shaw. Although Shaw's greatest gift was her brilliant, dynamic lectures that inspired audiences, she lacked real leadership ability. Shaw's connection to the WCTU also hurt her chances because many suffragists did not care to be aligned with temperance.

Lillie Blake had also served the suffrage movement well, but she lacked the charisma and popularity of Carrie Chapman Catt. Blake may have been popular among the inner circles of NAWSA's leaders, but few among the general membership knew her. She did not receive a high level of publicity from newspapers and journals, as other members did.

The third and most likely candidate, Carrie Chapman Catt, really did not want the job. Carrie claimed she had no desire to be president, yet she saw that opportunities would open up if she were to take on the office. She wanted the membership to value her organizational skills and, to an extent, reward her for the triumphs achieved by the Organization Committee.

Carrie also questioned whether she could afford to spend more time away from her husband. She did not want to stop her work with the Organization Committee, but she could not handle both the committee's work and the job of president. George Catt encouraged her to run for president, telling her not to worry about him or the money. George believed Carrie's rise to the presidency was a natural result of all the work she had previously done for the suffrage movement.

Alice Stone Blackwell, daughter of Lucy Stone and Henry Blackwell, immediately spoke out in support of Carrie. Lucy Stone had died in 1893, but Alice remembered her mother's deathbed wishes. In the February 17, 1900, edition of *The Woman's Journal,* Blackwell reported her mother's comments just before her death: "If Carrie Catt ever is a candidate for president of the national association, I hope all our Massachusetts people will vote for her, and I want you to tell them I said so." Fulfilling her mother's request, Alice Stone Blackwell fully supported Carrie for president.

Not too surprisingly, Susan B. Anthony's input provided the deciding factor in the election. Anthony loved Shaw like a daughter, but she recognized Carrie's leadership abilities and methodical approaches to work. After working closely with Carrie on lecture campaigns, Anthony knew that Carrie's sharp and innovative mind gave her the potential to be the best candidate. The election was quick and decisive. Not surprisingly, Carrie earned 254 of the 275 votes cast.

The NAWSA convention took place in Washington on February 8, 1900. Anthony stood before the crowded audience to introduce Carrie as the new president. The *Washington Post* reported Anthony's speech:

> I have the great pleasure of introducing Mrs. Chapman Catt as your choice for president. I never made a presentation with greater delight than this. From what I have seen of her work during the last decade, I am sure you have made a wise choice.

Realizing that she was on the verge of replacing a legend, Carrie stood breathless before the audience.

Anna Howard Shaw wanted to replace Susan B. Anthony as the president of the National American Woman Suffrage Association. *(Courtesy of the Library of Congress.)*

After taking a moment to herself, Carrie addressed the crowd:

> Good Friends, I should be hardly human if I did not feel gratitude and appreciation for the confidence you have shown in me, but I feel the honor of this position much less than its responsibility . . . I was not willing to be the next president after Miss Anthony. I have known that there was a general loyalty to her which could not be given to any younger worker . . . Miss Anthony will never have a successor.

Although Anthony and many members of NAWSA were happy to see Carrie elected, her new position created a serious split between the old members and the new. Only a few days before the election, the executive committee had agreed to continue Carrie's Organization Committee's support. Now, with Carrie as president, many committee members feared she would become too powerful as both president and chairwoman of the committee. A few days after her election, the executive committee of NAWSA voted to end the Organization Committee. This action angered many of Carrie's closest supporters, especially the volunteers she had personally trained on the Organization Committee.

Susan B. Anthony had given up the presidency, but she did not lose her power or prestige. Carrie found herself in the odd position of being the leader, yet having little say in actually leading or changing the association. Shaw, who had been Anthony's vice president, continued her position under Carrie. However, because of her loyalty to Anthony, Shaw always sided with the elder leader anytime a disagreement occurred between Anthony and Carrie.

During Carrie's first year as president, the United States faced another presidential election. NAWSA asked for time to speak at both the Republican and Democratic conventions. The Republicans gave up a mere ten minutes, while the Democrats refused to allow any suffrage speakers at all. William McKinley and Theodore Roosevelt represented the Republicans, and William Jennings Bryan and Adlai Stevenson ran on the Democratic ticket. None of these politicians was willing to address the suffrage issue.

Against all odds, Carrie decided to do what she could to make NAWSA more efficient. She struggled to increase the membership and bolster attendance at major meetings and conventions. Once again, Carrie became a tireless fund-raiser and organized a national suffrage bazaar in Madison Square Garden in New York City. The bazaar featured booths from every individual suffrage association selling goods from their home state. Louisiana offered pecans and pralines, molasses, and sugar cane. Utah sold silk by the bale. Florida brought oranges, grapefruits, and alligators. Booths offered displays of dolls, arts and crafts, quilts, blankets, and autographed photos of famous writers and artists. Kansas baked bread on site and sold it along with fresh churned butter.

Newspapers and journals sent reporters to cover the daily sales and nightly lectures. At night, crowds swarmed to the bazaar to listen to speakers on women's rights topics. Suffrage took center stage. In addition to building public relations, NAWSA earned about ten thousand dollars.

After much hard work and planning of events, Carrie Chapman Catt's first year in office ended with a tidy sum in the association's bank account. While NAWSA stood on solid financial ground, efforts to earn the vote stalled. Because no political party would support woman suffrage during the upcoming presidential election, Carrie and her fellow association members had little hope for passing a suffrage amendment in 1900.

For some time, Carrie had been considering the idea of an international suffrage association. For years she had wondered about woman suffrage in foreign countries. To Carrie's dismay, Susan B. Anthony immediately shot down her idea. Carrie was unaware that Anthony and Elizabeth Cady Stanton had tried to generate international interest in woman suffrage by starting the International Council of Women (ICW) in 1888. After two years, the council was still active, but suffrage was no longer its main focus. ICW's interests in 1900 covered everything from peace and education to putting flower boxes in classrooms. Anthony and Stanton left the council when a group of respected English women refused to support suffrage, an issue they considered too radical.

Undaunted, Carrie resolved to see what, if anything,

could be done on an international level. She created questionnaires and sent them to leading women from all over the world asking about the status of women in their countries. The form contained twenty-eight questions covering the rights of married and single women, educational opportunities, jobs and wages for women, divorce and custody rights, women's rights in the courtroom, and restrictions placed on women by society, parents, and husbands. Carrie received responses from thirty-two countries.

In light of the interest expressed through the questionnaires, Carrie helped found the International Woman Suffrage Alliance (IWSA) in 1902. Eight countries with woman suffrage societies sent delegates to the NAWSA annual convention. These representatives came from Australia, Denmark, Germany, Great Britain, Norway, and Sweden. Delegates from Chile, Hungary, Russia, Turkey, and Switzerland also arrived for the meeting. Carrie summed up the situation:

> The outlook for the vote was unpromising. Four states in the United States had given the vote to women and a lively organization was pushing on with brave determination. The situation was practically the same in Great Britain and the Scandinavian countries. The women could see small advantage in uniting their efforts and those who answered the first call to action were brave souls indeed.

With Carrie's help and determination, the international suffrage movement gradually made gains. As early as 1881, the Isle of Man had passed woman suffrage. New Zealand gave women the right to vote in 1893, and Australia in 1902. In Iceland, women held roughly twenty-five percent of the council positions in Reykjavík by 1902. In Sweden, tax-paying, unmarried women could vote in city elections but not in national elections.

In 1902, the National Education Association asked Carrie to speak at their annual meeting. She was the first suffrage leader to speak before the association. As usual, Carrie's speech enthralled the audience. She pointed out the educational advances of girls in the United States. Statistics were in her favor. More young women than ever before were attending colleges and universities. More girls graduated from high school than in previous generations. Carrie predicted that the United States would soon be a country that prevented its more learned citizens from voting.

Late in 1902, New Hampshire decided to vote on woman suffrage in an upcoming vote in March 1903. NAWSA had little hope of swaying New Hampshire, a highly conservative political arena. However, as Carrie knew, there could be no success without effort. In December, Carrie headed to New Hampshire to organize meetings, speakers, and workers. The season turned out to be the coldest winter she could remember. Suffering through the bitter weather, speakers traveled across the state in horse-drawn sleighs, wrapped in heavy blankets and warmed by hot bricks at their feet.

Despite a successful campaign, the amendment lost by over nine thousand votes. New Hampshire, like other states, suffered from political corruption. Carrie was upset but resigned herself to the fact that the suffragists had done their best in the face of adversity.

By her fourth year as president, Carrie suffered from poor health. Her mother and husband were also ill. To make life easier for George, the Catts sold their Brooklyn home and moved to Manhattan. They took a long vacation to Europe, one of the first occasions the couple spent significant time together. They toured Italy, France, and Switzerland. Travel relaxed Carrie, but George's stomach ailment did not improve, and Maria Lane, Carrie's mother, continued to get worse.

Carrie felt that the demands of the suffrage movement prevented her from caring for her family. She decided to resign and hand the presidency over to Anna Howard Shaw.

Carrie announced her resignation in the January 1904 issue of *The Woman's Journal:*

> I desire to announce the fact that I shall not stand for reelection to the presidency of the National American Woman Suffrage Association at the coming convention in Washington. The importance of the office required that careful consideration should be give to the election of my successor, and for this reason I make the announcement publicly and in due season.
>
> I have no intention of retiring from suffrage work,

although I find that a rest from the responsibilities of the office has become necessary. This alone is my reason for wishing to withdraw my name at this time. Whatever strength or ability I may have is first, last, and all the time consecrated to this cause, which is dearer than all others to me . . .

Although Carrie resigned as president, she agreed to serve NAWSA as Shaw's vice president. She also continued her interest in the International Woman Suffrage Alliance, now almost two years old.

Carrie attended the IWSA's annual convention in Berlin, Germany. It was an odd place to hold the conference, because German law prohibited women from attending public meetings about politics. The German suffragists avoided the law by organizing the meeting in Hamburg, a free city. A policeman attended the meeting, furiously scribbling notes about what each speaker said. Carrie, warned earlier about what she could and could not talk about, carefully chose her words. Women from a dozen countries attended the meeting.

Annie Furuhjelm, a newspaper editor from Finland, came to the meeting in hope of gaining recognition for Finnish women. The ICW had turned her down because Finland fell under Russian rule. In the early 1900s, czars still ruled Russia with an iron hand. No one voted in Russia—or Finland—while under the czar's control.

When no one would help Furuhjelm, she turned to Carrie. "I found her standing in a great hall full of people, watching calmly the whirl around her . . . She stretched out her hand to me, and I put the case of Finland before her. She was encouraging and most sympathetic." Carrie stood up for Finnish women and accepted them into the IWSA, despite the fact that their chance of success in gaining the vote was small. However, the IWSA executive committee was in for a surprise. Annie Furuhjelm turned out to be a whirlwind for the suffrage cause. Within a year, she organized the Finnish women, developed a campaign strategy, and emerged successful. On their first try, Finnish women became the first European women to gain the vote.

Chapter Six

The International Carrie Catt

Carrie spent most of 1904 caring for George, who suffered from gallstones, or calcium deposits in the gall bladder. During this time, gallstones were difficult to remove. The gall bladder attacks caused George terrible pain and weakness. In 1905, Carrie and George were sitting on a park bench when George suffered his final attack. An operation to remove the gallstones revealed that he also had a bleeding ulcer. Infection set in, and he died on October 8, 1905.

Carrie was crushed by George's death. She kept her distance from most friends while she mourned. Those who knew Carrie realized that she was seriously depressed by her loss. Her own health was even affected. Carrie took no interest in suffrage for a while. Because she could not stand to be in the Manhattan apartment that she and George had shared together, Carrie stayed in a hotel room.

In her sorrow, Carrie turned to her close friend Mary

Hay. Hay, known as "Mollie," became friends with Carrie while campaigning in New York, and the two had become very close over the years. Hay realized that Carrie needed to get back into her work in order to overcome her grief. It was the one thing that could occupy her mind.

Once Carrie recovered from the loss of her husband, she returned home, and Mollie Hay moved in with her. The two lived in the same home for many years and balanced each other's talents. Carrie was the outward face of suffrage; Hay was the diplomat behind the scenes. Together they made a dynamic, powerful team. They shared the same ideals: commitment to suffrage and dedication to women's rights. Carrie found in Hay someone whose work ethic and drive matched her own, although their relationship centered around more than suffrage and work.

After losing George the previous year, Carrie, along with her cohorts, had to deal with another loss. On March 13, 1906, Susan B. Anthony passed away after suffering from pneumonia and an ailing heart. Many women mourned as one of the founding members of the suffrage movement was now gone.

To get her feet back on the ground, Carrie attended the third IWSA convention in Copenhagen, Denmark. Women from more than a dozen countries affiliated themselves with the international group. The IWSA typically worked toward suffrage through peaceful means, but the 1906 conference attracted a group of militant reformers called "suffragettes" from England.

These British women belonged to the Women's Social and Political Union (WSPU), founded by Emmeline and Christabel Pankhurst. British newspapers had deemed the women suffragettes to distinguish them from the calm, peaceful suffragists. WSPU members frequently ended up in jail over the fervor of their protests.

The IWSA refused to recognize the WSPU because a British branch of the IWSA already existed. WSPU activities came under heated discussion. Some IWSA members felt that the WSPU's protests hurt the progress of the British suffrage movement, but Carrie admired the women's audacity. Others admired the WSPU's ability to gain press coverage of their antics.

Despite disagreement among the groups, the Copenhagen conference produced impressive results. Finnish women had succeeded in gaining universal suffrage for everyone twenty-four years of age and older. Norwegian women would get the vote within the next year, and Danish women earned voting rights in city elections. Even conservative England considered giving the vote to women householders, or women who ran homes on their own without male support. Compared to the United States, where no new states had passed suffrage since Idaho, the advances in Europe encouraged Carrie.

The following year brought more tragedy to Carrie's life. In the spring of 1907, she returned to Charles City, Iowa, to care for her mother, Maria. The time was stressful, but it provided Carrie with a chance to spend time with her younger brother, Will, who had recently returned from the Philippines. Will suffered from an unspecified nervous ailment, yet he seemed to be in reasonably good health. The reunited family spent many hours together, and Carrie watched her mother's health slowly improve.

Tragedy struck in September when Will took his wife to visit her parents in Illinois. During the stay, Will died suddenly. Stunned, Maria Lane fell into a steady decline from which she could not recuperate. She passed away on December 3, 1907. Within three month's time, Carrie had lost her brother and mother.

Grief-stricken, Carrie stayed in Iowa for two months until she had regained her composure. After attending suffrage hearings in Albany and Washington, Carrie headed to the Fourth Congress of the IWSA in Amsterdam. Suffrage in the United States remained stagnant under the ineffective leadership of Anna Howard Shaw, but European suffrage continued to advance. At the 1908 IWSA conference, representatives came from as far away as South Africa and Australia, and the press arrived in droves. A highlight of the meeting turned out to be a male delegate from Great Britain's Men's League for Women's Enfranchisement. Finland reported nineteen women serving in elected offices in the national government. Finally, the IWSA adopted a motto that all their members supported: *In necessariis unita, in dubiis libertas, in omnibus caritas* (In essentials unity, in nonessentials liberty, in all things charity).

During the conference, women throughout England marched on London's Albert Hall to show their support for woman suffrage. A violent meeting at Parliament Square a few days later landed more than two dozen suffragettes in jail. Carrie praised these women for their courage.

Many smaller suffrage groups formed in the United States. Carrie saw this as an opportunity to unite some of the smaller New York groups into one political faction: the Woman Suffrage Party (WSP). Carrie and Mollie Hay worked together to develop the party. Carrie provided the strategy; Hay became the outward face of the WSP.

In 1909, Harriot Stanton Blatch, daughter of Elizabeth Cady Stanton, invited Emmeline Pankhurst of England's WSPU to speak before the first conference of the Woman Suffrage Party. Pankhurst, a British suffragette, openly advocated militant action to gain women voting rights. Her various jail sentences and overt protests made her famous. Pankhurst spoke to a packed crowd in New York City's Carnegie Hall.

The following week, another suffrage conference met in Carnegie Hall. This meeting included suffrage representatives from throughout New York. Carrie's new strategy was to combine forces and use the WSP as a political weapon. A council presented the party's strategy for gaining women the right to vote in New York. For years, New York politicians ignored the activities of the suffrage movement. They saw no threat from a group of organized women who could not vote. The WSP, however, was a force to be reckoned with. New York politicians took open notice of the woman suffrage movement, now organized and working in the same political venue that they themselves occupied. This was an exciting time for Carrie, although her health suffered. For some time, Carrie had been suffering from migraine headaches, bouts of exhaustion, and generally poor health. When the 1909 conference took place in London, she attended fewer functions and met with fewer people than ever before. The endless travel drained what little energy she had left.

Carrie, now fifty years old, said she suffered from anemia, or low levels of iron in the blood. Following doctor's orders, she retired to New York's Catskill Mountains for the summer of 1909, intent on taking a "rest cure." In the early 1900s, doctors recommended rest cures for a variety of illnesses, ranging from depression to physical exhaustion to tuberculosis.

Despite the extended rest, Carrie's health did not improve. By the spring of 1910, she was bedridden. Her doctor ordered her to strengthen her body by eating large amounts of food at frequent intervals, but Carrie's thoughts focused more on dying than getting well. Her physical symptoms and mental depression kept her away from suffrage activities. Mollie Hay grew concerned about her friend's failing health but could do nothing to help her.

By June, Carrie's heart had weakened and she underwent an operation of an unspecified nature. Her doctor recommended another full year of rest, to which Carrie answered that she would take a trip around the world. Carrie recorded her thoughts on her "rest year" in her journal:

> There were three things that I had to do before I could start. I was president of the International Woman Suffrage Alliance, a congress was due soon in Stockholm, and it was my duty to prepare the program and do the correspondence with our auxiliaries. I must preside over the congress and when the congress should be over, the minutes and records had to be prepared and printed. My doctor, hearing about these tasks, said solemnly, 'Then you must rest two years, instead of one.'

Carrie and Mollie Hay set sail for Europe and the Stockholm conference in June 1911. The number of countries supporting the IWSA now reached two dozen. At the conference, Carrie pointed out the growing worldwide economic problems that forced women from their homes and into the workplace. Women worked alongside men, did the same jobs as men, yet they earned far less than their fellow male workers.

Within two weeks, Carrie was free to take her worldwide rest tour. Her traveling companion was Aletta Jacobs, a long-time friend and fellow suffragist. Although Carrie planned to rest on her trip, she could never fully leave the suffrage movement behind. When their ship docked in Cape Town, South Africa, Carrie planned to enjoy some sightseeing. She also wanted to meet with members of the two African suffrage groups that were members of the IWSA. During her seventy-six-day visit in Africa, Carrie made forty-five speeches at luncheons, high teas, dinners, and other meetings. Overall, sightseeing and suffrage work balanced out to thirty-six days of touring and forty days of campaigning.

During her hectic stay in South Africa, Carrie met Mohandas Gandhi. At the time, Gandhi was living in Johannesburg. As an Indian, Gandhi was scorned by those who resented his attempts to gain better treatment for his fellow Hindus. In the future, he would lead a massive civil rights movement in India. Carrie had no idea at the time that Gandhi's peaceful resistance to oppression would thrust him into worldwide fame: "His eyes lighted with an inner fire and he spoke with such fervor that we recognized that we were in the presence of no ordinary man . . . The impression that remained was that I had for the first time in my life seen a genuine fanatic."

While Carrie was in Africa, California passed a law allowing women to vote. The news thrilled Carrie, who recognized the importance of California to western states. Continuing with the vacation, Carrie and Jacobs boarded a ship in Durban, South Africa, and headed up Africa's east coast toward the Middle East.

Throughout her trip, Carrie encountered women from varied cultures. She was very curious to learn how women of other cultures participated in the women's rights movement. She questioned the veils Muslim women wore in public, and she worried about the lack of education of many Middle Eastern women.

In Ceylon (now Sri Lanka), Carrie observed families working on tea plantations in slave conditions. She confronted the plantation owners about their employees. She was told that the tea pickers were happy with their work and lifestyles. Carrie coldly responded that she had heard the same said about the contentment of wives, but only as spoken by their husbands.

Throughout their visit to India, Carrie and Jacobs could not help but notice the difference between the wealth of the Indian royalty, called rajahs, and the poverty of the common people. The caste system, under which the Indian people divided themselves into distinct social classes, puzzled the visitors, as did many of the customs of a land so different from their own. Repeated inquiries produced no information about any woman suffrage or any women's rights movements at all in India. Nevertheless, persistence paid off, and Carrie did meet a number of women trying to bring about social reform in India.

These women had little interest in voting rights, as their problems were much different from European or American women's difficulties. Instead, they fought to end child marriages, improve women's wages, and increase educational opportunities for women.

Of all the places Carrie visited, she found China the most fascinating. She and Jacobs attended a meeting of revolutionaries in Canton and discovered that there were many women in important positions among the rebels. Carrie was excited to find that women of the revolution expressed themselves openly and voted according to their own thoughts. She described the experience in her diary:

> The women wore trousers like all the other women in China. The men wore light colored garments, the women were in black except one who wore blue, and at least two of them had bound feet. The members did not address the chair to gain the floor, but simple rose and began to talk . . . The vote was taken by rising, and we noticed that the lady members did not always vote the same way.

In Shanghai, Carrie found an active women's rights movement. Some of the women had fought in the revolutionary armies of China and now wanted social and political freedoms equal to those of Chinese men. She offered the members of the Women's Cooperative Association of Shanghai an opportunity to join the IWSA. The group became the first Far East members of the alliance.

Throughout her trip, Carrie encountered intelligent, educated women; poverty-stricken women; women with few freedoms; and women fighting for many freedoms. Her travels spanned several continents and took her across the world's oceans. Yet, she realized that in many ways, women shared many connections. They all wanted the best for their children, freedom for their daughters, and a better way of life for themselves.

Chapter Seven

The World, the War, the Presidency

After women in California gained the right to vote in 1911, Arizona, Kansas, and Oregon followed suit. At this point, women had equal voting rights with men in ten states. Carrie vowed not to stop campaigning until every state supported universal adult suffrage.

Upon her return to New York in 1912, Carrie attended a suffrage meeting in Carnegie Hall in November. She spoke of her trip and the common goals of the women she had met. Carrie presented a picture of women on the verge of rebellion—women fighting for freedom in humble villages and huge cities against old laws and traditions. "This battle for equal justice is not for ourselves alone," Carrie said. "Our cause is one." The audience rose up in applause. When Carrie finished her speech, Mollie Hay asked for donations. In all, Carrie and Hay raised five thousand dollars that evening.

Illinois and New York became primary targets for the suffrage movement. Both had large populations and dynamic business communities. Success in Illinois and New York would lead to success throughout the country. In 1908, President Theodore Roosevelt had told suffragists that they should turn their tactics to a state other than New York. By 1913, no politician dared make such a statement. With Carrie's devotion, the suffrage movement had become a strong political force, overwhelming, irresistible, and constantly moving forward. Carrie left the United States to attend the 1913 IWSA meeting in Budapest. On her way there, she spent two weeks in England. Carrie had just learned that the Alaska Territory and the state of Illinois had passed woman suffrage amendments, and she was elated by the news. The victory in Illinois was particularly important, considering the size of the population and the economic impact of Chicago on the Midwest.

In England, the violence connected to the woman suffrage movement struck Carrie. Suffragettes, the more militant suffrage workers, lit fires, broke windows, and staged hunger strikes. In retaliation, the British government jailed the violent suffragettes. Those on hunger strikes had tubes pushed into their stomachs and were forced to eat. The more the government threatened, the larger the protest rallies became.

Emmeline Pankhurst was jailed and freed repeatedly. In the House of Commons, the prime minister claimed to have no knowledge that women were truly interested in the vote—despite thirty thousand people in favor of woman suffrage gathering only a few miles away in Trafalgar Square.

The size and power of the suffrage movement in England thrilled Carrie, although the amount of violence concerned her. She worried that many opposed the quarrelsome nature of the suffragettes more than they opposed suffrage itself. Criminal acts, such as arson and vandalism, would only increase the stubbornness of the opposition. Still, Carrie could not help but be impressed by the extent to which British women went to secure the vote. The May 31, 1913, issue of *The Woman's Journal* reported Carrie's description of London's atmosphere, "The suffrage campaign in the United States is a dull and commonplace affair when compared with the sizzling white heat of the British struggle."

Carrie regretted leaving London, but Budapest and the IWSA awaited her arrival. The conference filled the meeting halls. The largest conference yet, more than 2,800 people attended. Now recognized around the world, the IWSA drew 230 reporters, and newspapers from around the world printed coverage of the meeting.

The press presented several interesting stories about the conference. Major speeches were recorded on gramophone records. The recordings would allow suffragists and women's rights activists to hear the speeches even if they had not attended the meeting. The IWSA now had members on five continents with the addition of the Chinese women's group. Finally, a group of Transylvanian peasants arrived at the conference on foot, having walked from Romania to Budapest. These women desperately wanted the vote and worked indus-

These women hang posters supporting woman suffrage in New Jersey, 1914.
(Courtesy of the Library of Congress.)

triously to earn that right. Within five years, Transylvania had granted universal adult suffrage.

The demands of state, national, and international suffrage efforts once again drained Carrie's energy. She planned to retire as president of the IWSA because so much work was needed in the United States. At the meeting in Budapest, she handed the office to someone else. Members of the alliance moaned over their loss. German suffragist Frau Lindemann begged Carrie to rethink her plans: "Dear Carrie Catt, you have many splendid workers in America, and you can give the greatest part of your time to your country. We have only you!" The argument did not change Carrie's mind—New York needed her.

The Budapest conference would be the last IWSA conference for some time. In the summer of 1914, an assassin's bullet would throw the world into war. The assassination of Austria's Archduke Francis Ferdinand in Sarajevo lit a fuse that exploded into World War I. At the time, many European countries had formed military alliances with each other. Germany, Austria-Hungary, and Bosnia declared war on Serbia, the home nation of Ferdinand's assassin. Great Britain, Russia, and France supported tiny Serbia. Suddenly, European countries, with few exceptions, were at war. Although the United States chose to remain neutral, German torpedoes sank U.S. ships, including passengers liners crossing the Atlantic.

The women's movement in Europe would have to wait as women fought to stay alive. The desire to vote seemed a minor issue compared to men dying in trenches, mustard gas, and fields filled with endless rows of graves.

In New York, women joined together to protest the war. More than two thousand black-clad women marched in New York City in August. The atmosphere was somber, quiet, and emotional. Carrie took a more sensible approach to the war, proposing that the organized women of Europe be called upon to pursue peace. Although she believed that the march would not change anything in Europe, Carrie also donned mourning black and walked with her colleagues.

A number of well-known women promoted peace by various means. Rosika Schwimmer, a famous IWSA activist from Hungary, came to the United States with a lengthy petition asking President Woodrow Wilson to help negotiate peace. In the United States, social reformer Jane Addams and industrialist Henry Ford decided to go to Europe on a "Peace Ship" with the goal of stopping the war. Although the two had a positive goal in mind, this idealistic venture was doomed from the start. Ford invited dozens of famous people to join him and Addams, but few saw any merit in the plan.

While the rest of the world struggled through World War I, the United States suffrage movement kept up its momentum. A new election campaign with the slogan, "Victory in 1915," became front-page news as suffragists planned their strategies in New York, Pennsylvania, New Jersey, and Massachusetts. Using her renowned organizational skills, Carrie conceived a plan for New

York that would literally leave no voter in ignorance.

Carrie used a new approach in New York: a school for suffrage volunteers. Carrie's school taught the basics of suffrage, including the workings of the government, public speaking, women's history, and politics. Support for the New York movement swelled as New York City's Woman Suffrage Party membership reached a total of more than one hundred thousand people.

The effort to sway New York voters covered every aspect of public life. Carrie said:

> The City campaign was more intensive than in any other part of the State, as its political unit organization had been established longer and therefore worked more smoothly. There were barbers' days, days for firemen, street cleaners, bankers, brokers, business men, clergymen, street car men, factory workers, students, restaurant and railroad workers, ticket sellers and choppers, lawyers, ditch diggers and longshoremen. No voter escaped.

Despite the activities of the New York campaign, the women fought an uphill battle. As always, conservative thinkers, politicians in office who feared women gaining power, and the ever-present liquor industry opposed women having the right to vote. Again, no political party would support the suffrage amendment. Despite Carrie's great efforts in the state, New York's amendment lost by 194,984 votes.

Neighboring state campaigns fared equally poorly.

Many who opposed woman suffrage argued it would lead to the breakup of the family structure. *(Courtesy of the Library of Congress.)*

In New Jersey, the liquor lobby and powerful Democratic leaders opposed the amendment as well. Many anti-suffrage women also spoke out against the amendment, and New Jersey's amendment lost by 51,108 votes. Pennsylvania's campaign made use of the Liberty Bell and Independence Hall as a backdrop to women's rights. Nonetheless, Pennsylvania voters also rejected woman suffrage with 441,034 votes opposed to the amendment.

The final 1915 referendum took place in Massachusetts. The state's women avidly supported suffrage, but political thinking remained conservative. Again, woman suffrage lost. The Massachusetts loss posted the greatest defeat by percentage: only thirty-six percent of the voters favored the amendment.

Although the woman suffrage amendment had failed in four states, Carrie saw a bright side to the defeat. Woman suffrage had earned over one million favorable votes in only four states. The immediate result might have been depressing, but the future outlook promised victory.

The end of 1915 marked the end of an era. In December of that year, the United States Senate and the House of Representatives introduced Bill #1, which would add a woman suffrage amendment to the U.S. Constitution. While suffragists cheered the move, one particular activist realized that the bill announced a greater battle than woman suffrage had ever fought before. Dr. Anna Howard Shaw, president of NAWSA, decided that she did not want to take on the amount of work needed for the campaign. Admitting her inability to carry out such a demanding task, Shaw announced her resignation as president.

Carrie and Mollie Hay headed to Washington, D.C., for the next NAWSA convention. In their minds, many excellent leaders were available to replace the retiring Dr. Shaw. They had no idea whom the general membership favored. Not surprisingly, the majority wanted Carrie Chapman Catt—everyone except the New York membership and Carrie herself. A great deal of maneuvering forced the New Yorkers to give Carrie up to the national movement. The New Yorkers wanted her to continue working closely on gaining suffrage in their state. They could not afford to lose her leadership.

Although Carrie chose to decline her election, the members of NAWSA drafted her into taking the position. Carrie accepted the job, but not graciously. "I am an unwilling victim," she told her audience at the meeting. She did not want the job, and she resented having it forced upon her. Carrie's acceptance speech struck the membership like a slap in the face:

> Now I'm old, I'm unhealthy, and I'm tired out, but I will do my best! . . . I have a right to demand in return for my acceptance that, if you have any complaint about the conduct of the association or that of the board, you will bring your complaint first to us. Let us get together and sink differences. Let us call upon those psychological sources of strength innate in all of us. Let organization be the watchword of the year.

It has been my hobby for the last hundred years . . .
I have come to my task in an appalling state of
unpreparedness. I will do my best, but you must all
give me your help. Let us work harder this year than
ever we have before. Let us make our slogan, "Get
together."

Chapter Eight

War on Two Fronts

The suffrage movement began achieving well-earned success throughout the country. In 1916, three states—Iowa, South Dakota, and West Virginia—planned to vote on suffrage. A national law, Bill #1, was slated for discussion in Congress, and a presidential election would be held in November. Support for woman suffrage was on the rise, and Carrie remained optimistic. She spent the first half of the year campaigning as much as possible, trying to regain any momentum she felt she had lost since her presidency ended twelve years before. Overall, she visited twenty-three states. Despite Carrie's persistence as president, 1916 proved to be a year of deceit, crisis, and disappointment.

The first vote took place in Iowa, where once again, suffrage lost due to heavy activity in liquor interests. Further investigation uncovered some erratic practices on the part of many election districts. In some places, polling officers failed to keep a record of how many people actually voted. In other districts, unused ballots "disappeared" so that no accurate record could be made. Polling lists that did exist did not compare accurately with the number of votes cast. Even worse, the state had no means to recount or address voting irregularities in an amendment issue. Overall, forty-seven violations of Iowa's election laws had occurred, and nothing could be done to change the result.

Carrie scolded her home state:

> Iowa, one of the most intelligent and progressive states in the nation, stands at the bar of public opinion accused of incapacity to conduct an honest election. How she will defend herself, what reparation she will make to her women, and what steps she will take to insure clean elections and better enforcement of her election law in the future are problems which await the Legislature.

In South Dakota, citizens voted on woman suffrage and prohibition of alcohol in the same election. Prohibition won; suffrage lost. Carrie was livid at the all-too-familiar circumstances surrounding the vote. The vast majority of voters opposing suffrage were German-Russian, many of whom could neither speak nor read English. Many foreign-born voters were not even citizens, as all that was needed for a man to vote in South Dakota were entrance papers into the country.

West Virginia became the closest state to the South to even consider voting on woman suffrage. Carrie

A suffragist dressed as *Liberty* marches on the steps of the capitol.
(Courtesy of the Library of Congress.)

said, "The illiteracy rate of the state is appallingly high and the illiterate is universally an anti-woman suffragist . . . Election Day came. Women poll workers reported from many parts of the state that drunken hoodlums were marched in line into the precinct, saying boldly that they were going to vote 'agin the women.' " Not surprisingly, woman suffrage lost in West Virginia.

With a presidential election in the fall, Carrie hoped to have a woman suffrage policy added to each political party's election platform. She again organized national suffrage action with the precision of a military campaign.

Resistance remained high. The liquor lobby pushed hard to stop woman suffrage, certain that a victory for women would mean a victory for prohibition. In the South, politicians fought against any change that would take power away from white males. Conservative politicians in the East were so stuck in the past that no amount of prodding would move them.

Under Carrie's leadership, the NAWSA Congressional Committee wrote proposals for each party to endorse woman suffrage. In Washington, suffragists lobbied congressmen and political leaders to ensure that the woman suffrage proposals would be included in party plans.

Carrie realized that promises made in Washington carried little weight away from the capital. Thus, in every state and every voting district, women organized to guarantee that politicians would keep their promises. Delegates from the national association planned rallies and marches in Chicago and St. Louis, where the upcoming political party conventions would be held. On the morning of June 7, rain poured down on the streets of Chicago. Carrie and her fellow suffragists did not let this stand in their way. More than fifty-five hundred women proceeded in raincoats and rubber boots, marching through the streets of Chicago to the convention hall. The suffrage issue tore through the Republican Party with equally staunch supporters on the pro and con sides. In the end, negotiations resulted in a carefully worded statement of minimal support: "The Republican Party reaffirming its faith in government of the people, by the people, and for the people as a measure of justice to one-half the adult people of this country favor the extension of the suffrage to women, but recognize the right of each State to settle this question for itself."

The Progressive Party openly supported woman suffrage, but their power was limited. The Progressives' strength lay mostly in states that had already given women the right to vote. The Democratic Party followed the Republican pattern, issuing a statement that loosely supported woman suffrage based on state-by-state acceptance.

The executive board of NAWSA immediately responded by declaring a state of emergency and moving their annual November convention to September 1916. Woodrow Wilson, president and Democratic candidate, and Republican candidate Charles E. Hughes received invitations to attend. Although Hughes declined, Wilson wisely did not. He stood before the convention and said, "I have come to fight not for you but with you, and in the end I think we shall not quarrel over the method."

Wilson was reelected as president, and hopes rose that the woman suffrage amendment would have a hearing in the joint houses of Congress. On April 2, 1917, Congress met in a special session to discuss the possibility of going to war. The war in Europe was closing in on the United States. The first order of business was to be the woman suffrage amendment, and Carrie sat in the gallery to hear the debate. Instead of woman suffrage, President Wilson asked Congress to decide whether or not to declare war on Germany, which had continued to torpedo American merchant vessels in the Atlantic.

Carrie knew that war would make demands on the nation's women. She recognized that war consumed vast resources, such as men, money, and materials. She knew that the war would overwhelm even the most active suffrage campaign. Although she did not want to allow the war effort to stall the suffrage movement, Carrie realized that she had little choice but to support the war.

With the country at war, President Wilson called on many people to support the war effort. He asked Carrie Catt and Anna Howard Shaw to be part of the Women's Committee of the Council of National Defense. Carrie considered working for the war to be one of her duties as a citizen. She also recognized the value in supporting politicians and knew the contacts she made in Washington could only help the suffrage cause.

Before a hearing for a woman suffrage amendment could be scheduled, Woodrow Wilson (here with his wife, Edith) prepared the nation for entry into World War I. *(Courtesy of the Library of Congress.)*

The members of the Women's Committee represented the most powerful women's groups of the time: suffragists, temperance groups, social service clubs, and groups with historical leanings, such as the Colonial Dames. Through their connections, these leaders could approach nearly every woman in the United States. Anna Howard Shaw, known by all the women, became the chairwoman, while Carrie was to research and report on foreign women and what they were doing to help the war effort in their countries.

The first meeting of the Women's Committee took place in Washington, D.C., in May 1917. The women had no offices or meeting rooms. They scrambled to find chairs once they finally found a meeting place. They were eventually assigned to an old, empty theater. The women quickly arranged the space into meeting rooms and offices.

A food crisis loomed on the horizon in the United States. Canned foodstuffs, meat, and dairy products were being shipped overseas to support the troops. Those on the home front needed to find a way to supplement food in the average household. The Women's Committee suggested that women plant vegetable gardens across the country. They encouraged women to dry foods (beans, peas, and apples, for example) and can vegetables and fruit. Women's magazines printed recipes for meatless, wheatless, and butterless meals. Women were also asked to knit socks, make bandages, and work in factories.

Women flocked to factory jobs, taking their places

as metal workers, machinists, and assembly line workers. As they worked, these women still had responsibilities in the home. The Women's Committee urged women not working in factories to open daycare centers and support local schools. Carrie's work on the Women's Committee paralleled her work for suffrage. She traveled extensively, meeting excessive demands to speak, meet, and confer with government, labor, and suffrage groups. On a typical day, she gave two or three speeches, attended an equal number of meetings, and then traveled to her next destination.

Carrie, now close to sixty, volunteered to travel to Canada in May to see how women in that country supported the war effort. She attended to war matters in Toronto, then returned to the United States to tour midwestern and western states on suffrage business. At the Mississippi Valley Suffrage Conference in Columbus, Ohio, Carrie said:

> Our nation is engaged in the defense of democracy; the hearts of women would beat more happily if they could feel that our own Government had been true to the standard it proposes to unfurl upon an international field.

> We speak not so much for ourselves as in defense of our republic, in hope that it will resume its historic place as leader of democracy. We demand the suffrage by Federal amendment in the United States as a war measure!

To Carrie's frustration, Congress refused to discuss any bills or issues except war efforts during its session. In retaliation, suffragists pushed harder for a Woman Suffrage Committee to be formed in the next session of Congress. This idea had two main advantages. First, it took the suffrage issue out of the hands of the conservative Judiciary Committee, whose members strongly opposed the suffrage amendment. Second, it drew attention to suffrage as a major issue before Congress.

Once again, suffrage campaigning led Carrie back to New York. She still considered the state a primary target. Her long-time companion, Mollie Hay, still led the Woman Suffrage Party in New York. The party's numbers and strength had continued to grow, and in 1917, the amendment had a fair chance to pass. A New York City political society, known as Tammany Hall, had many members whose wives had joined the suffrage cause. In support of their family members, Tammany Hall proclaimed that the amendment should go to vote in a clean election, without any cheating or pre-arranged votes.

Carrie led a massive pre-election march in 1917 in favor of woman suffrage, just as she had done two years earlier. This time the women from upstate New York carried petitions with more than five hundred thousand signatures in favor of the suffrage amendment. The New York City organization had gathered a similar number of signatures, putting the total beyond one million. Election day arrived, and the amendment passed in New York. Celebrations erupted throughout the state.

Women suffragists picket the White House in 1917.
(Courtesy of the Library of Congress.)

Carrie and Hay were jubilant as years of effort had paid off at last.

NAWSA continued to organize women at every level, from national efforts and state organizations to local polling districts. In 1917, because of Carrie's methodical organization, women in Michigan, Ohio, Indiana, North Dakota, Nebraska, Rhode Island, and New York won the right to vote in presidential elections. Vermont gave women the right to vote in city elections.

In December, the national convention of NAWSA met in Washington, D.C. During the meeting, many of NAWSA's leaders reported to Carrie that their states would support woman suffrage. Carrie could see victory on the rise. Very pleased, she stepped to the podium to give her presidential address:

> It has been the aim of both dominant political parties to postpone woman suffrage as long as possible. Many of us have a deep and abiding distrust of all political parties; they have tricked us so often that our doubts are natural. We also know that your parties have a distrust of new women voters. Woman suffrage is inevitable—you know it . . . Shall we, then, be enemies or friends? There is one thing mightier than kings or armies, congresses or political parties—the power of an idea when its time has come to move.

It was a bold move. In the midst of World War I, Carrie Chapman Catt had declared war on a second front: woman suffrage versus the U.S. Congress.

Chapter Nine

The Final Thrust

World War I ended in Europe in 1918, but the battles for suffrage raged on in the United States. The woman suffrage movement, under the guidance of NAWSA President Carrie Chapman Catt, steamrolled across the country. Three days after the war's end, Carrie was already busy making plans for the next IWSA meeting.

The total number of fully enfranchised women was now over seven and a quarter million in fifteen States. And so successful had been the work for presidential suffrage that these seven and a quarter million full-fledged voting women were flanked by eight million more who could vote for president in twelve other states . . . The day of triumph of the Federal Suffrage Amendment was at hand.

Women from every state camped out in Washington, D.C. They formed a continuous, ever-present lobby in the Capitol. No senator or representative passed through the Capitol halls without hearing NAWSA's message.

Carrie knew that passing a woman suffrage amendment would be a three-step process. Initially, each branch of Congress would debate and vote on the amendment. If the amendment passed both the House and Senate, it would need to be ratified by three-fourths of the states. Carrie arranged for suffragists to lobby politicians throughout the process.

In the House of Representatives, a new Suffrage Committee met, despite attempts by Democrats to slow down the process. The committee scheduled a hearing to debate the suffrage issue. Carrie described the tension of the hearing in her own words:

> Men rose to make interminable speeches on man's God-given right to tell woman what she must and must not do . . . They rose to speak with force and fire in an effort to make other men forsake old fashions of autocratic thought and feeling and espouse fundamental democracy . . .
>
> Down on the floor and out in the cloakrooms tottered men so ill that they should have been in bed, but on hand at any hazard to vote for suffrage. Enthusiasm could not be repressed when the Republican leader, James R. Mann, of Illinois walked feebly to his seat. Everybody knew that he had left a hospital in Baltimore to answer the suffrage roll-call. Another man, who was in such pain from a broken shoulder that he wandered about cloakrooms and corridors like a soul

possessed, was in his seat on the Democratic side, just the same, when his name was called.

Victory in the House required a two-to-one vote in favor of the amendment. On May 21, 1919, 393 members of the House of Representatives voted on the woman suffrage amendment. With 304 men in favor of the vote, and only eighty-nine opposed, the amendment passed in the House. After seventy years of constant effort, the woman suffrage amendment was on its way to victory. Capitol corridors filled with laughing, crying, singing women, jubilant over the victory. "Many a member who had voted 'no' was seen with hat pulled low over his eyes, listening as he hastened toward the exit–perhaps comprehending that on that day a new thing had come to the nation," said Carrie.

In the Senate, the debate over the woman suffrage amendment began during a dreadful hot spell in early June. Suffragists again filled the galleries and lined the hallways. Carrie decided to stay home to save herself the trouble of sitting through more congressional speeches. Again, a two-thirds majority was needed to pass the amendment. The roll-call vote began late in the afternoon. After a final tally, the "ayes" totaled fifty-six, while the "nays" had only twenty-five. The suffragists had won. Mollie Hay, who had attended the congressional meeting, phoned Carrie immediately to give her the good news.

After the House and Senate passed the amendment, it still needed to be ratified by the states. This was one of Carrie's greatest achievements. The massive nation-wide organization she had created once more set its wheels in motion. Each state already had a ratification committee thanks to Carrie's prior planning long before the suffrage amendment was on the congressional slate. She sent telegrams to the chairwomen of each ratification committee telling them to get moving. If their state legislation was in session, Carrie wanted to see ratification immediately.

Illinois and Wisconsin ratified the amendment within a week, with Illinois becoming the first state to pass the amendment. Michigan followed within hours. Within another week, Kansas, New York, and Ohio added themselves to the list. Pennsylvania, Massachusetts, and Texas ratified the amendment within the first month. By the end of the summer, seventeen of the required thirty-six states had ratified the Nineteenth Amendment. The suffragists had almost reached the halfway point.

As part of Carrie's strategy, she told suffragists not to let the amendment come to a vote in any state in which the result was in question. Her experience in the suffrage movement told her that victory followed upon victory. The last thing the amendment needed was a defeat to stall its forward momentum.

During this period, Carrie proposed an idea she had considered for many years: the League of Women Voters. She knew that many women lacked political knowledge and decided the best way to overcome this deficiency was through a league dedicated to teaching women about voting and politics. Carrie saw the league as a temporary solution to be used until women were sufficiently schooled in their new civic opportunities. In October, Carrie decided to head west on a "Wake Up America" tour. At that point, five of the fifteen states that had already granted full suffrage had ratified the amendment. Carrie's goal was to prod the remaining states into taking positive action. The tour was lobbying at its highest level. She hit thirteen states in eight weeks in her usual nonstop fashion. During the trip, she pushed for ratification and presented the idea of the League of Women Voters.

Late fall brought success in five more states. Nine additional states ratified the amendment in early 1920. Not every state, however, voted for the amendment. The South, in particular, strongly opposed woman suffrage. The amendment initially failed in Mississippi, South Carolina, Virginia, Delaware, Georgia, and Alabama.

NAWSA decided to hold a Victory Convention in Chicago in February 1920. Although the amendment still had not been fully ratified, suffrage leaders felt renewed confidence in their success. At the convention, Carrie explained the nature and purpose of the League of Women Voters. The primary goal of the league would be education, not party politics.

Those who attended the convention awarded Carrie with a diamond and sapphire brooch to commemorate her service to woman suffrage. Supporters from all across the country had contributed nickels and dimes to pay for the piece of jewelry. It was a parting gift to a woman who had given her life to the suffrage cause.

With only one more state needed to finally ratify the Nineteenth Amendment, Carrie and her crew set their sights on Tennessee. The final battle was not easily won. The suffragists were scorned, cursed, and threatened. Carrie herself received letters so vile and offensive that she could hardly believe the thoughts came from sane people. When the ballot finally arrived, men were once again taken from hospital beds, whisked off trains, and brought to the state capitol to cast their votes.

The vote came to a tie at forty-eight to forty-eight. Twenty-four-year-old Harry T. Burn, a first-term representative from Tennessee and also the youngest member of the legislature, had intended to vote against the amendment. Before Burn announced his decision, he read a note his mother had written to him: "Vote for suffrage . . . Don't forget to be a good boy." When his name was called, Burn voted "Yay." The suffrage amendment had passed.

On August 26, 1920, U.S. Secretary of State Bainbridge Colby announced the passage of the Nineteenth Amendment to the U.S. Constitution. After more than forty years devoted to the cause of woman suffrage, Carrie Chapman Catt felt the pure joy of victory. She and her fellow suffragists paid a visit to President Wilson at the White House to give him a special gift from NAWSA acknowledging his hard work for the cause of suffrage. Carrie then left immediately for a celebration in New York the following day.

When she arrived, Carrie was met by an enormous

crowd of suffragists, photographers, and reporters. Women waved banners and clapped their hands for the woman they hailed as their almighty hero. Carrie, as ecstatic as her fans, remarked upon the event: "This is a glorious and wonderful day. Now that we have the vote, let us remember that we are no longer petitioners. We are not the wards of the nation but free and equal citizens."

After the amendment had passed and Carrie had some free time to herself, she retreated to her new home at Juniper Ledge, New York, with Mollie Hay. Carrie wanted to relax, exercise, and attend to activities around her yard, such as planting and building a greenhouse. She still gave occasional speeches for various women's groups around New York and spent time researching legal matters surrounding anti-suffragists.

The Nineteenth Amendment ended the suffrage movement in the United States, but many women in other countries still wanted the vote. World War I had shut down the suffrage cause in Europe, and resuming the International Woman Suffrage Alliance after the war proved difficult. Bitter feelings of the women of the Allied nations against women from Germany, Austria-Hungary, and other Central Powers created a major obstacle for Carrie and the IWSA.

The first post-war conference took place in Geneva, Switzerland. Over four hundred women attended the Eighth Congress of the IWSA. Every country sent delegates except Belgium. The women assessed their situation in Europe and found that the war had actually helped the women's movement. New national borders brought many women into countries that had already granted women the right to vote. Ten countries had women in their legislatures. Women played significant roles in setting up governments in newly formed Czechoslovakia, Poland, Latvia, Estonia, Lithuania, and the Ukraine. In the Crimea, Muslim women not only voted, but they also held five seats in the national congress.

Carrie also heard a number of disheartening speeches at the conference. Women from different countries talked of problems such as starvation, inflation, political instability, and increasing violence towards women. "Facing the gigantic political tasks, the newly won vote seems pitifully poor and small," Carrie remarked.

Carrie had big plans for the IWSA. She hoped that the Alliance would strive for universal adult suffrage throughout the world, but that was just a start. She wanted the IWSA to be a global force for peace. Now that the war had ended and women had won the vote in the U.S., Carrie wanted to turn her eyes on a broader vision of women as a united political force for social reform and everlasting peace.

To bring about this global force, Carrie needed to pull the remaining countries into the IWSA. She initiated a fact-finding venture to learn about marriage and the rights of married women, employment and fair treatment of women in the workplace, healthcare for women and children, and the moral character of various nations. The IWSA created committees to research each of these areas.

Carrie wanted the IWSA to investigate the status of women in South America, the only continent in the world that did not allow women to vote. Through the League of Women Voters, Carrie and Lavinia Engle from Baltimore, Maryland, planned a Pan-American conference open to all Latin American countries. At the conference, the women created a new alliance: The Pan-American Association for the Advancement of Women. Carrie became the association's first president, but only for a year.

During that first year, Carrie also worked with Nettie Shuler to write *Woman Suffrage and Politics: The Inner Story of the Suffrage Movement.* The book covered the complete history of the suffrage movement in the United States. As Carrie recalled old NAWSA campaigns, she found herself reliving past frustrations. The book became an outlet for Carrie's pent-up anger over the deceit and underhanded actions of anti-prohibition supporters, self-serving men, and malicious politicians.

Carrie now found herself pulled between the IWSA and the Pan-American Association. She felt as if she were forever on a boat between Rome and Panama, or Great Britain and Latin America.

The 1923 IWSA convention brought Carrie to Rome, the heart of Italy. Benito Mussolini, Italy's leader, welcomed the IWSA in a speech that Carrie considered condescending. He gave token acceptance to woman suffrage by offering a minor degree of suffrage in local or city elections. After so many years of dealing with politicians, Carrie's diplomatic grace had evaporated.

She responded to Mussolini with little patience: "Men tell us that you stand for order, for unity, for patriotism, for a better and higher civilization in the world. These are our ideals, too . . . We make no political intrigues. We shall not disturb the peace of Italy. We have, however, asked all the civilized Governments of the world to endorse our plea and our program."

The 1923 conference became a defining point in Carrie's life. At that point, she felt that she had done more than enough for the women's movement. Success in the suffrage movement grew worldwide. It was time to turn her attentions to a far more worthy cause: world peace. In 1925, she led the first meeting of the Committee on the Cause and Cure of War.

More than four hundred delegates attended the first convention, held in Washington, D.C. The delegates debated the various causes of war, pinpointing roughly 250 direct and indirect causes. The committee's primary goals were to educate people about peace and to negotiate nonmilitary solutions to disagreements among countries. The committee actively lobbied Congress to pursue peaceful solutions in dealing with other countries.

From 1925 to the beginning of World War II in 1939, the committee continued to advance the cause of peace. Carrie openly voiced her opinion that war solved nothing, destroyed much, and should become a marker of things past. The committee avoided dwelling on the horrors of past wars and instead tried to find a way to end the political and economic factors that pushed men into war. She said: "Men have been taught that physical courage is a man's chief virtue. [If a man avoids a fight] some one is sure to call him a coward. We women have no such obstacle in our way."

Unfortunately, the Committee on the Cause and Cure of War failed. Carrie no longer had the energy needed to push the committee's platform forward. She served as president from 1925 through 1932. During that time, political and social factions that disagreed with Carrie attacked her committee and its efforts. Still, she seemed unconcerned by the strife swirling around her. Different factions, such as the American War Mothers, openly criticized her peace plans. Others, such as the International League for Peace and Freedom, appeared to agree with Carrie's committee, but they actually disapproved of the committee's means to achieve a lasting peace.

In 1928, Carrie left city life behind. She had reached the age of sixty-nine and needed to retire. Carrie bought a house in New Rochelle, New York, a half-hour train ride from New York City, and moved in with Mollie Hay. The house was spacious, with sunrooms, a large living room, a library, and enough wall space for Carrie to hang her collection of photographs, letters, and documents from her days in NAWSA.

On Mollie Hay's seventy-first birthday, August 29, 1928, Carrie had planned a great celebration. The two were dressing for the party when Carrie realized that Mollie's normal chatter from the next room had stopped. She found her friend unconscious on the bed and immediately called a doctor. A medical exam indicated a burst blood vessel in the brain. Hay died only hours later.

The death of her closest friend shocked Carrie. She bought a double cemetery plot in nearby Woodlawn Cemetery. After the funeral, Carrie seemed sick at heart. An old family friend from Iowa, Alda Wilson, came for a visit. Although she had not planned to stay very long, Wilson moved into Carrie's New Rochelle home permanently.

Over the next years, Wilson pleaded with Carrie to moderate her activities, but Carrie refused. After such a hectic and full life, "retirement" was simply not part of her plans. She missed Mollie Hay and filled the emptiness left by Hay's death with visits, trips, and meetings.

By 1939, all hopes of world peace ended when Germany invaded Poland on September first. Carrie served as honorary chair of the Women's Action Committee for Victory and Lasting Peace. She wholeheartedly supported the international venture. She wanted peace in the world above all else.

During World War II, Carrie devoted her energies to helping Jewish refuges and European suffrage leaders, many of whom lived in exile because of Hitler's sweeping progress across Europe. From her New Rochelle study, she sent letters, wrote pamphlets, and organized petitions for the exiles' relief. She was among the first to inform the United States political leaders of the truth about Hitler's cruel treatment of Jewish people in concentration camps and in the Warsaw ghetto which brought death to so many.

Carrie Chapman Catt retired to her New Rochelle home after a lifetime of fighting for women's rights. *(Courtesy of the Library of Congress.)*

At the war's end, Carrie, eighty-five, spent most of her days in her library. She continued to receive visitors regularly and even traveled when she could. On March 8, 1947, at the age of eighty-eight, Carrie spent the day as she would any other, reading, writing, and talking with her visitors. Sometime after midnight that night, Carrie suffered a heart attack. On the morning of March 9, Carrie was pronounced dead. After a simple funeral, she was buried beside Mollie Hay. The memorial over their graves reads, "Here lie two, united in friendship for thirty-eight years through constant service to a great cause."

Timeline

1859—Carrie Lane is born in Ripon, Wisconsin.

1880—Graduates from Iowa State Agricultural College.

1883—Becomes the first woman to be appointed superintendent of schools in Mason City, Iowa.

1885—Marries Leo Chapman; they run the *Mason City Republican.*

1886—Leo Chapman dies from typhoid fever in San Francisco.

1887—Joins the Iowa Woman Suffrage Association.

1890—National and American associations for woman suffrage merge to become the National American Woman Suffrage Association (NAWSA); Carrie Chapman marries George Catt.

1892—Speaks at the NAWSA annual convention in Washington, D.C.

1893—Colorado votes in favor of woman suffrage, becoming the second state to allow women to vote.

1900—Succeeds Susan B. Anthony as president of the NAWSA.

1902—Helps form the International Woman Suffrage Alliance.

1915—Returns to lead NAWSA after several years abroad; Anna Howard Shaw resigns as president of the NAWSA, and Catt becomes the president again.

1917—NAWSA supports the war effort under Catt's
     leadership.
1919—League of Women Voters is founded.
1920—Nineteenth Amendment to the Constitution is ratified,
     giving women the right to vote.
1923—Publishes *Woman Suffrage and Politics: The Inner
     Story of the Suffrage Movement.*
1925—Founds the Committee on the Cause and Cure of War.
1947—Carrie Chapman Catt dies in New Rochelle, New York.

Sources

CHAPTER ONE: Rural Beginnings

p. 19, "How is it possible that a woman . . ." *Charles City (Iowa) Intelligencer,* 28 June 1877, 2.

p. 20, "We were . . . twice as big as Carrie Lane . . ." Jacqueline Van Voris, *Carrie Chapman Catt: A Public Life*(New York: The Feminist Press, 1987), 10.

p. 22, "Few young people start out . . ." Mary G. Peck, *Carrie Chapman Catt: A Biography* (New York: The H.W. Wilson Company, 1944), 39.

CHAPTER THREE: A Time of Change

p. 35, "We made a team . . ." Carrie Chapman Catt, "A Suffrage Team," *Woman Citizen* (September 8, 1923): 11-12.

p. 36, "At one place where I took three meals . . ." Carrie Chapman Catt, as quoted in the *New York Times,* 19 March 1911, sec. V, 8.

p. 38, "Not one of them could speak English . . ." Carrie Chapman Catt, from an undated speech in the Schlesinger Library Archives.

p. 43, "Startled by their own victory . . ." Carrie Chapman Catt and Nettie Rogers Shuler, *Woman Suffrage and Politics:*

The Inner Story of the Suffrage Movement (New York: Scribner's, 1923), 119.

CHAPTER FOUR: Learning to Lead

p. 45, "The ballot is the weapon . . ." interview with Carrie Chapman Catt, *New York Times*, 14 January 1894, 12.

p. 47, "The largest auditorium in the city was packed . . ." Peck, *A Biography*, 79.

p. 48, "the most heart-breaking defeat of the suffrage struggle." Van Voris, *A Public Life*, 41.

p. 50, "Suffrage is today the strongest reform . . ." Ibid.

p. 56, "Faithful watchers . . ." Catt and Shuler, *Woman Suffrage and Politics,* 123.

CHAPTER FIVE: Madam President

p. 60, "If Carrie Catt ever is a candidate for president of the national association . . ." *The Woman's Journal*, (February 17, 1900).

p. 60, "I have the great pleasure of introducing . . ." "The Washington Convention," *The Woman's Journal* (March 3, 1900): 67.

p. 62, "Good Friends, I should be hardly human . . ." Ibid.

p. 65, "The outlook for the vote . . ." "The Early Days of the Alliance" *The International Women's News* (April 1935): 54.

p. 67, "I desire to announce the fact that I shall not stand . . ." *The Woman's Journal*, (January 1904).

p. 68, "I found her standing . . ." Van Voris, *A Public Life*, 63.

CHAPTER SIX: The International Carrie Catt

p. 76, "There were three things . . ." Carrie Chapman Catt in her fifth diary of her world trip, Library of Congress.

p. 77, "His eyes lighted with an inner fire . . ." Carrie Chapman Catt, "A Glimpse of Gandhi," *The Woman's Journal* (March 25, 1922): 13.

p. 79, "The women wore trousers . . . " Peck, *A Biography*, 198.

CHAPTER SEVEN: The World, the War, the Presidency
p. 80, "This battle for equal justice . . ." Van Voris, *A Public Life*, 106.
p. 82, "The suffrage campaign in the United States . . ." *The Woman's Journal* (May 31, 1913.)
p. 84, "Dear Carrie Catt . . ." Peck, *A Biography*, 209.
p. 86, "The City campaign . . ." Catt and Shuler, *Woman Suffrage and Politics*, 288.
p. 89, "I am an unwilling victim," Van Voris, *A Public Life*, 130.
p. 89. "Now I'm old, I'm unhealthy . . ." Peck, *A Biography*, 237.

CHAPTER EIGHT: War on Two Fronts
p. 92, "Iowa, one of the most intelligent . . ." Carrie Chapman Catt, *Woman Suffrage by Federal Constitutional Amendment* (New York: National Woman Suffrage Publishing Co. Inc., 1917), 41.
p. 94, "The illiteracy . . ." Ibid., 46.
p. 95, "The Republican party . . ." Catt and Shuler, *Woman Suffrage and Politics*, 253-254.
p. 96, "I have come to fight . . ." Ibid., 260.
p. 99, "Our nation is engaged . . ." Peck, *A Biography*, 273.
p. 102, "It has been the aim . . ." Ibid., 283.

CHAPTER NINE: The Final Thrust
p. 103, "The total number of fully enfranchised women . . ." Catt and Shuler, *Woman Suffrage and Politics*, 315.
p. 104, "Men rose to make . . ." Ibid., 321.
p. 105, "Many a member who had voted 'no' . . ." Ibid., 322.
p. 108, "Vote for suffrage . . ." Geoffrey C. Ward and Ken Burns, *Not for Ourselves Alone: The Story of Elizabeth Cady Stanton and Susan B. Anthony* (New York: Alred A. Knopf, 1999), 224.
p. 109, "This is a glorious and wonderful day . . ." Van Voris, *A Public Life*, 162.

p. 110, "Facing the gigantic political tasks, the newly won vote . . ." Ibid., 170.

p. 112, "Men tell us . . ." Catt and Shuler, *Woman Suffrage and Politics,* 179.

p. 113, "Men have been taught . . ." Ibid., 199.

Bibliography

Charles City Intelligencer, June 28, 1877.

"The Early Days of the Alliance," *The International Women's News,* April 1935.

American History Desk Reference. New York: Macmillan, 1997.

The Oxford Children's Book of Famous People. New York: Oxford University Press, 1999.

Borkman, Frances M., and Annie G. Poritt, eds. *Woman Suffrage: History, Arguments, and Results.* New York: National Woman Suffrage Publishing, 1915.

Catt, Carrie Chapman, and Nettie Rogers Shuler. *Woman Suffrage and Politics: The Inner Story of the Suffrage Movement.* New York: Scribner's, 1923.

Catt, Carrie Chapman. *Diaries.* Library of Congress.

———. "A Glimpse of Gandhi," *The Woman's Journal,* March 25, 1922.

———. "Good Friends . . ." speech, "The Washington Convention," *The Woman's Journal,* March 3, 1900.

———. "The Lie Factory," *The Woman Citizen,* September 20, 1924.

———. *New York Times,* January 14, 1894.

———. *New York Times,* March 19, 1911, part V.

───. "Poison Propaganda," *The Woman Citizen,* May 31, 1924.

───. "A Suffrage Team," *The Woman Citizen.* September 8, 1923.

───. Undated speech, Schlesinger Library Archives.

───. *Woman Suffrage by Federal Constitutional Amendment.* New York: National Woman Suffrage Publishing Co., Inc., 1917.

Catt, Carrie Chapman, et al. *The Ballot and the Bullet.* Philadelphia: A.J. Ferris, 1897.

Fowler, Robert Booth. *Carrie Catt: Feminist Politician.* Boston: Northeastern University Press, 1986.

Miller, Helen Hill. *Carrie Chapman Catt: The Power of an Idea.* Washington, D.C.: Carrie Chapman Catt Memorial Fund, 1958.

Peck, Mary G. *Carrie Chapman Catt: A Biography.* New York: The H.W. Wilson Company, 1944.

Somervill, Barbara A. *Ida Tarbell.* Greensboro, N.C.: Morgan Reynolds, 2002.

Van Voris, Jacqueline. *Carrie Chapman Catt: A Public Life.* New York: The Feminist Press, 1987.

Ward, Geoffrey C., and Ken Burns. *Not for Ourselves Alone: The Story of Elizabeth Cady Stanton and Susan B. Anthony.* New York: Alred A. Knopf, 1999.

Collections and Associations

Catt, Carrie Chapman. Collected papers, Library of Congress

Center for the Historical Study of Women, Binghamton University/SUNY

League of Women Voters

National American Woman Suffrage Association. Collected Papers, Library of Congress

National Women's History Project

Susan B. Anthony Center for Women's Leadership, University of Rochester

Websites

Carrie Chapman Catt Childhood Home
http://www.catt.org

Welcome to the Carrie Chapman Catt Center for Women and Politics at Iowa State University
http://www.iastate.edu/~cccatt/homepage.html

National Women's History Project
http://www.nwhp.org/

A History of the American Suffrage Movement by Doris Weatherford
http://www.suffragist.com/timeline.htm

Index

Addams, Jane, 85
American Association of
  Women, 23
American Equal Rights
  Association, 28
American Woman Suffage
  Association (AWSA), 28,
  30, 34, 39
Anthony, Susan B., 28, *29*,
  30, 34, 39-40, 45, 49-50,
  55, 58, 60, 62-64, 71

Blackwell, Alice Stone, 39,
  41, 46, 59-60
Blackwell, Henry, 30, 59
Blake, Devereaux Lillie, 58-59
Blatch, Harriot Stanton, 74
Burn, Harry T., 108

Campbell, Margaret, 32
Catt, Carrie Lane Chapman,
  childhood, 9-10, *11*, 12,
  14-15
  death, 116
  education, 14-16, 18-19

lectures, 31-32, 35-36, 46-
  47, 49-50, 55, 66, 80,
  99, 102, 107
marriage, to Leo Chapman,
  20, 22, 24, *25,* to
  George Catt, 31, 35,
  39-40, 48, 53-54, 67, 70
president of NAWSA,
  (1900), 58-60, 62-64,
  66-68, (1915), 89-92,
  94-95, 102-103, 106-
  108
sickness, 39, 67, 75-76
as teacher, 16, 18-20, *21*
and world peace, 112-114,
  116
Catt, George, 31, 35, *37*, 39-
  40, 48, 53-54, 59, 67-68,
  70-71
Chapman, Leo, 20, 22-24, *25*,
  39
Columbia Exposition of 1893,
  40
Committee on the Cause and
  Cure of War, 112-113